LANNY M. TRON, ESQ.

I met D. J. Vodicka seven years ago when he asked me to represent him in a lawsuit against the California Department of Corrections for unlawful retaliation. He had blown the whistle on a gang of rogue guards that were abusing prisoners, planting evidence, and covering up their misdeeds. Unfortunately, his whistle-blowing was not applauded by other prison guards or the wardens. Instead, D. J. was ostracized and he even received death threats. In fact, he had to go into hiding for his own safety. When we first met all he wanted was to get his life back, but they were not willing to do so. I tried to help him reclaim his life and to expose the Green Wall.

D. J.'s book The Green Wall is a truly riveting story of a California prison guard who blew the whistle on corrupt guards that abused their power in the nation's largest prison system. The story is a firsthand account that provides a rare look into a world of murderers, molesters, and gang members sequestered behind twenty-foot concrete prison walls. The book describes D. J.'s trials and tribulations both as a prison guard and a private citizen. I trust you will enjoy reading it as much as I enjoyed living it.

Respectfully yours,

LANNY M. TRON
LAW OFFICES OF LANNY M. TRON

It is very unusual for police and corrections officers to put their lives on the line to expose brutality and corruption in their own departments. That is exactly what D. J. Vodicka did in his career and now currently doing in an even bigger way, in writing his story The Green Wall. By following protocol and adhering to the policies put in place by his department, D. J. soon found out that rules were intentionally being broken and specific policies were purposely neglected. The more he tried to adhere to his profession's ethical standards, the greater the retaliation became and he eventually he lost everything. We need more brave and ethical officers like D. J.; and we need law enforcement agencies to adhere to their policies on truthfulness, excessive force and ethics.

Chief Penny E. Harrington
Former Chief of Police, Portland, Oregon
Founding Director, National Center for Women & Policing
Expert Witness, Employment Discrimination

Everyone should be concerned about "America's Brutal Prisons;" as from behind "The Green Wall," comes out THE MOST POWERFUL EXPOSE EVER by X-Prison Guard, D J Vodicka, on the worst prison systems in the world. They are NOT built nor intended to rehabilitate, but instead, behind it all, lays one of the greatest "experiments" on human psychology, behavior, slave labor, torture, and mind-control.

How can it be that the people, who are in control today, are actually more criminal and more sinister in their behavior, than the very people that they are supposed to house and "protect"? May God Help, "our" helpless prisoners in America today, who are now reduced to being captured "chattel" property and legally DEAD, while approximately seventy percent of those who are in prison today are actually INNOCENT of having committed any real crime!!!

So now that the REAL Truth is "known," who will go after the REAL criminals who are standing there holding those precious keys over Life and Death.

Thank You D. J. Vodicka, our Number One Prison Guard in America Today, for being so brave and coming out, while Breaking their C-O-D-E- of silence; YOU are Truly An American Hero! No American, nor anyone else for that matter, deserves to be T.o.r.t.u.r.e.d..., EVER.

Dezert-owl, Survivor of Torture
Int'l Radio Host/ Producer of www.TheREALPublicRadio.Net
We Are ALL Doing Time!

THE GREEN WALL

A PRISON GUARD'S STRUGGLE TO
EXPOSE THE CODE OF SILENCE IN
THE LARGEST PRISON SYSTEM IN
THE UNITED STATES

D.J. VODICKA

iUNIVERSE, INC.
NEW YORK   BLOOMINGTON

The Green Wall
The story of a brave prison guard's fight against corruption
inside the United States' largest prison system

iUniverse books may be ordered through booksellers or by contacting:

iUniverse
1663 Liberty Drive
Bloomington, IN 47403
www.iuniverse.com
1-800-Authors (1-800-288-4677)

Because of the dynamic nature of the Internet, any Web addresses or links contained in this book may
have changed since publication and may no longer be valid.

ISBN: 978-1-4401-4059-4 (sc)
ISBN: 978-1-4401-4057-0 (dj)
ISBN: 978-1-4401-4058-7 (ebk)

Library of Congress Control Number: 2009936993

Printed in the United States of America

iUniverse rev. date: 10/12/2009

THE GREEN WALL

A PRISON GUARD'S STRUGGLE TO
EXPOSE THE CODE OF SILENCE IN
THE LARGEST PRISON SYSTEM IN
THE UNITED STATES

D.J. VODICKA

iUniverse, Inc.
New York   Bloomington

The Green Wall
The story of a brave prison guard's fight against corruption inside the United States' largest prison system

iUniverse books may be ordered through booksellers or by contacting:

iUniverse
1663 Liberty Drive
Bloomington, IN 47403
www.iuniverse.com
1-800-Authors (1-800-288-4677)

Because of the dynamic nature of the Internet, any Web addresses or links contained in this book may have changed since publication and may no longer be valid.

ISBN: 978-1-4401-4059-4 (sc)
ISBN: 978-1-4401-4057-0 (dj)
ISBN: 978-1-4401-4058-7 (ebk)

Library of Congress Control Number: 2009936993

Printed in the United States of America

iUniverse rev. date: 10/12/2009

A whistleblower can be defined as a person who reveals any wrongdoing taking place within an organization. A whistleblower can make a disclosure of corruption, mismanagement, illegal activities or any other wrongdoing. It is an unavoidable fact that persons who step up as whistleblowers are often then faced with retaliation from their employers. There are Federal as well as State regulations and statues that have been put in place in order to protect whistleblowers from any kind of retaliation that they might have to face.

California Whistleblower Act

The Legislature finds and declares that state employees should be free to report waste, fraud, abuse of authority, violation of law, or threat to public health without fear or retribution. The Legislature further finds and declares that public servants best serve the citizenry when they can be candid and honest without reservation in conducting the people's business. "Protected disclosure" means any good faith communication that discloses or demonstrates an intention to disclose information that may evidence in an improper or governmental activity or any condition that may significantly threaten the health or safety of employees or the public if the disclosure or intention to disclose was made for the purpose of remedying that condition. An employee may not directly or indirectly use or attempt to use the official authority or influence of the employee for the purpose of intimidating, threatening, coercing, commanding, or attempting to intimidate, threaten, coerce, or command any person for the purpose of interfering with the rights conferred pursuant to this section.

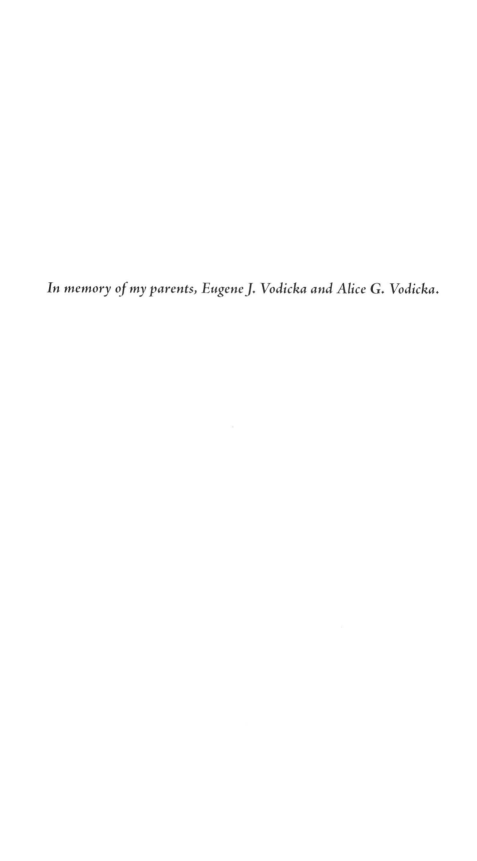

In memory of my parents, Eugene J. Vodicka and Alice G. Vodicka.

ACKNOWLEDGEMENTS

First and foremost, I would like to thank my wife, Marian, for her continuous love and support through not only this stressful ordeal, but for also staying by my side during the passing of my mother and father.

I would also like to thank my very special and best friend, Joseph Reynoso, for his dedication while training me when employed with the California Department of Corrections and Rehabilitation. To him and his wife, Les, I am forever grateful for their belief in me and their constant support.

Thank you, to attorney and true friend, Mr. Lanny Tron, who once said to me, "One day you will be able to tell your son that you are a true hero, you have the courage to stand up for what is right and you can pass this on to him." You Lanny are a true hero in my eyes.

Many thanks to my editor, Jillian Bruno.

Lastly, I want to express thanks to my closest friends, Dr. Timothy Little and his wife Shari Little. Thank you Tim for your time and efforts in creating my website: www.greenwall2001.com. Thank you both for your hospitality, kindness and friendship.

BIOGRAPHY OF THE AUTHOR

DONALD J. VODICKA, ("D. J.")

Donald J. Vodicka, ("D. J.") was born on March 5, 1962, in Camarillo, California. Raised by two wonderful parents, Eugene J. Vodicka and Alice G. Vodicka, D. J. had a passion for law enforcement at a young age. At the age of twenty-one, D. J. enlisted in the United States Army. In 1988, after serving four years on active duty, he entered the California Department of Corrections and Rehabilitation in Galt, California. Just three months later, he was assigned to his first prison, the famous, Corcoran State Prison.

Vodicka's admirable work ethic and reputation furthered his honorable career in law enforcement. He held positions With Corcoran State Prison, Calipatria State Prison, Pelican Bay State Prison, Salinas Valley State Prison and Pleasant Valley State Prison; all maximum state prisons in California. They house the most violent felons and gang members in the state.

On January 20, 2004, his exposure of the Green Wall in the Senate testimony, created a change in policy and procedures within the California Department of Corrections. It sanctioned mandatory additional training every year for all state employees. Vodicka also helped introduced two new state bills, which were passed to protect whistleblowers from reprisal or retaliation.

Both nationally and internationally, his story has gained the attention of numerous media outlets. The British Broadcasting Company featured a documentary called, <u>America's Brutal Prisons</u>, which has been showing in film festivals all over the world

Millions of prisoners, ex-prisoners, and prisoner's families comprise an extensive advocacy network on the internet. D. J. Vodicka's website on *The Green Wall* story is becoming a popular and important site for these people. The website, www.greenwall2001.com, provides an in-depth view on his ordeal, with newspaper articles, photographs, video clips, audio excerpts, and further background information.

Vodicka currently resides in the United States, but does not wish not to disclose his location.

FOREWORD

By
Edward Caden, Esq.
Chief Deputy Warden (Ret)
California Department of Corrections

Salinas Valley State prison was opened in 1996 by the California Department of Corrections as a state-of-the-art maximum security prison, designed to house 4,400 inmates. Having spent close to a quarter billion dollars on the design and construction of this new prison, the executive management of the department unfortunately paid little attention to ensuring that there was a proper and functioning management team in place to operate the new prison. The management team assembled was dysfunctional and more interested in power struggles and turf wars among themselves than to pay attention to the inmates and the officers, sergeants and lieutenants who dealt with the population twenty-four hours a day.

Without proper guidance and support from the management team, the officers felt that they were on their own. It became an "us against the inmates" mentality. Respect for the rule of law and the oath the correctional officers had taken to uphold and enforce the law had gone by the wayside. The disturbing mindset of the line staff is captured by a phrase commonly used at that time: "What goes on in the yard space stays on the yard." A Code of Silence was active among the staff and tolerated by the management. Senior departmental management turned a blind eye to the dysfunctional management team at Salinas Valley even as the level of violence in the prison continued to rise at a disturbing rate. Attacks against correctional officers have become commonplace. The officers, many of whom had had just graduated the academy, were ill-prepared to deal with the maximum security inmates they were charged with supervising.

Without guidance and support it became commonplace for the officers to take matters into their own hands and began to abuse inmates. That only fostered further violence. On Thursday, November 26, 1998, Thanksgiving Day, a dysfunctional prison unraveled and became a prime example of the decline of ethics among correctional officers. On this Thanksgiving Day, the *Green Wall* emerged.

Correctional Officer D. J. Vodicka was on duty that day, a member of the Investigative Services Unit—an elite, hand selected group of peace officers who were experienced investigators and handled major crime scenes for the prison. Officer Vodicka handled the crime scene of the Thanksgiving Day riot after approximately twenty-eight Hispanic inmates attacked staff on D Facility at Salinas Valley State Prison in Soledad, California. Eighteen correctional staff were injured, with fourteen treated at community hospitals.

As a sign of solidarity following this major riot, officers began wearing enameled turkey pins on their uniforms, signifying that they had survived the Thanksgiving Day riot. Later, other staff took to wearing the turkey pins as a sign of solidarity with their fellow officers. Some of the officers began to refer to themselves as the Green Wall—in recognition of the green uniforms worn by peace officer staff. The Green Wall members began engaging in serious and sterling misconduct, carving the numbers "7/23"—standing for the seventh and twenty-third letter of the alphabet, G and *W*—or the initials "GW" on walls, furniture, lockers, and other state property. Vandalism then morphed into physical and mental intimidation of inmates. Staff did not support the unprofessional conduct they were observing.

Incidents of inmate abuse grew and eventually came to the attention of Officer Vodicka. Vodicka could not tolerate the unprofessional and illegal conduct that he was observing and he reported the misconduct through the chain of command. His report however, was not met with an appropriate response by the department's management. Officer Vodicka was transferred to another prison while investigations were conducted. The newly appointed warden at Salinas Valley State Prison considered Vodicka "disloyal" and a "rat" for having filed complaints about the conduct of his fellow officers.

The department's Office of Internal Affairs investigated the complaints and concluded that there was no misconduct and no Green Wall. The independent Office of the Inspector General (OIG) however, conducted their own investigation and found that not only was there a group of staff known as the Green Wall, but several of its members had committed both administrative and criminal misconduct that included providing perjured testimony in court and planting weapons on inmates as evidence. The OIG submitted its report to the department and to the recently appointed warden at Salinas Valley for appropriate disciplinary and criminal prosecution of the involved staff. The department's management and the warden took no action.

D. J. Vodicka was labeled a rat among staff, was subjected to a constant barrage of harassment both on and off duty, and labeled disloyal by the management. Labeling him disloyal was quite inaccurate. He was loyal to the people of the State of California and to the law—that he took an oath to uphold. State law and department policy mandated that whistleblowers shall not be subjected to reprisals for filing complaints; however, department management—by their actions—showed that they could care less about law and policy by the way they treated D. J. Vodicka. The department management's unspoken, but clearly communicated message, was that loyalty to the department and to the people you work with—even if that means lying to conceal their misconduct—is valued over doing what is legally right and ethical.

In January 2004, when D. J. Vodicka and his attorney testified before a California State Senate committee about the Green Wall and the abuse he had suffered, the department could no longer hide. The warden suddenly went on "sick leave" and orders were given by top management to clean up the mess at Salinas Valley.

D. J. Vodicka paid an enormous price for coming forward and reporting misconduct—it ended his career. When he later sued the department, only in depositions given for the case did the truth begin to emerge about the abuse he suffered for reporting misconduct. The department, represented by the Office of the Attorney General—likely out of fear of public disclosure of the deep-rooted misconduct D. J. had revealed—settled the case. But even with the settlement D. J. was permanently injured and justice was not served.

D. J. Vodicka is a model of what happens to be an honest cop confronted with a dishonest agency. He gave the best years of his life living up to the high values and standards of professional conduct expected of him. His agency, the California Department of Corrections, let him down and in doing so, the California Department of Corrections let the people and the state of California down as well as the Constitution.

It is only by bringing D. J. Vodicka's experiences to light that the public can know what goes on behind the walls of our prisons, remembering that the Department of Corrections carries out its mission on behalf of and in the name of the people of the state of California. The public expects that its laws will be enforced professionally and humanely by the correctional officers it employs. Hopefully, D. J.'s experiences will bring about long-term change and one day restore a positive image to the profession D. J. served so well as a peace officer.

Introduction

In a single generation, America's prison population quadrupled, making us the world's leading jailer. More than one in every one hundred Americans are behind bars today, compared to one in one thousand forty years ago—an increase so explosive it has cost the nation over three trillion dollars to contain it. The incarceration boom was led by California, where more people are imprisoned per capita than anywhere else worldwide. It was here where I saw first-hand how prisons have become a dysfunctional institution, factories of violence run by savage gangs on *both* sides of the law.

My career encompassed not only this rapid expansion but the blurring line between good and evil. For sixteen years I worked as a guard in California's highest security prisons, serving meals to gang bosses and serial killers in lockdown cells and patrolling yards filled with the world's most violent felons. I belonged to the elite Investigative Services Unit, responsible for solving horrific crimes that took place inside the prison walls. While employed with the original *supermax* prison—a nickname for maximum security prisons—Salinas Valley State Prison, I was a decorated veteran with senior stripes when I blew the whistle on a secret gang of corrupt, sadistic guards who called themselves the *Green Wall*.

My story, *The Green Wall*, is the true and still unfolding drama of my fight to uphold the integrity and honor of the law enforcement system against a corrupt California state prison that turned against me for revealing the truth. My actions where further challenged as the government and media failed me at every turn, putting me and my family's life at risk.

Ordered by the warden of Salinas Valley State Prison and the Internal Affairs Unit, I was to secretly report ongoing atrocities committed by my own colleagues—a prison guard gang calling themselves the Green Wall. My efforts to expose the Green Wall gang were betrayed by the prison warden himself and his superiors.

I was labeled a snitch and ostracized, my career destroyed, my marriage ruined, and my life threatened so often that I was forced into hiding. Only reluctantly did I make my story public and become a government witness.

My story is a classic tale of personal integrity in the most dishonest place imaginable, of courage amidst brutality. It parallels the story of Frank Serpico; the New York City cop who exposed corruption in the city's police department in the 1970's and became the subject of the classic book, *Serpico*. Reading his story during my exile inspired me, while giving me the courage to come forward publicly, as Serpico did.

My televised state senate testimony exposed a scandal that led to terminations, sudden retirements, and a restructuring of the system that is still underway. In 2005, I won a whistleblower lawsuit against the California Department of Corrections. Prison guards are employed under non-disclosure contracts that normally prevent them from telling their stories, but I was exempted from this restriction as part of my settlement. This victory has allowed me to share my story.

> *"You have to stand tall when you stand alone. You have to stand tallest when no one else will stand at all. You can't ignore the truth."*
>
> *- D. J. Vodicka*

CHAPTER ONE

THE GREEN WALL

What Joe Reynoso called "The special parking area for law enforcement vehicles" was really just a side street with especially obvious No Parking/Tow Away signs every twenty feet, conveniently close to the California State Capitol Building. It was bordered by busy offices but patrolled vigilantly by the Sacramento Police Department. I followed Joe's unmarked but state-issued cavalier into the little street, then pulled over to park behind it. I felt my ulcer starting up as soon as I turned off the engine. Joe walked back to my muddy vehicle and stated, "You ready to do this?" I guess, I muttered as I got out of the car.

"You can't take your weapon into the Capitol D. J."

I sighed as I removed the Glock and holster from my belt. It was a weapon for someone confident in their ability to handle it and in my case, genuinely afraid for their life—hollow-point bullets, one in the chamber, no safety. I had slept with it for the last six months and practiced every day, firing off a thousand rounds a week at my mountain hideout.

My long time friend and colleague Joe Reynoso and my attorney Lanny Tron stood next to me outside the California State Capitol. I was nervous, and it was written all over my face.

Naturally, my appearance looked like the bad-guy wrestler the crowd loves to hate. At six feet, six inches tall and three hundred pounds, a shaved head and broad frame, I looked and lumbered like a pro-football lineman. From years working in the prison systems, my disposition was solid, emotionless and unreadable, except for today. I had worked for the state of California for sixteen years but had never been inside its Capitol building before. Together, the three of us set off toward the Capitol.

Near the southeast end of the building, a dozen TV news vans and crew members hauled equipment into the senate chambers. I figured this was standard, as there must regularly be important news to report from the Capitol. Reynoso and Tron new differently, but kept their silence.

At the entrance, I was thoroughly searched for any weapons I could have been carrying, while Reynoso—who was heavily armed—showed his credentials and entered through a discrete, separate gun port. Even with heightened post-9/11 security, there was nowhere in California that Joe wasn't allowed to carry his concealed weapons. For this reason, he accompanied me to court.

I stopped just short of the tall double doors of the governor's office, where a group of California Highway Patrol troopers in tailored uniforms stood at attention. I fantasized for a moment about dropping in to share my story with Schwarzenegger, who promised during last fall's campaign to put a lid on runaway prison costs. I thought the "Governator" might be interested in my grim story.

The hearing was scheduled for nine o'clock that morning and a large crowd was already waiting outside the courtroom, which surprised my attorney Lanny. He had expected something more private like the other administrative hearings—lawyer-like arguments around a conference table. Instead, there was a rude scramble for seats as soon as the bailiff opened the doors. My trial turned out to be the day's hot ticket in Sacramento; a joint session of the Senate Select Committees on Government Oversight and the California Correctional System. It was chaired respectively by Democrats Jackie Speier of San Francisco and Gloria Romero of Los Angeles. There were other members of both committees but none with much enthusiasm for looking closely at my prison situation, so they only made perfunctory appearances. It was basically a two-woman show.

Once inside the prestigious Burton Room, I was overwhelmed with its massive size and the people rushing through the doors. There were two hundred theater-style seats rising up from the floor with another two hundred on a wrap-around balcony level. All were filled in ten minutes after the doors were opened.

Speier opened the proceedings by waving a copy of that morning's *Los Angeles Times*, the state's biggest newspaper.

"Much of the testimony we will hear today will be startling and even unbelievable," she proclaimed. "Whistleblowers who speak under oath fear for their jobs and their lives."

I squirmed unnervingly; beneath a bold headline on the front page of the paper was a massive photo of me followed by an article:

> **Guard Challenges Code of Silence:** *Today, Donald Joseph Vodicka will stand before a state Senate committee on prison reform not as a guard but as a whistleblower. Instead of a career*

marked by commendations from wardens and prosecutors, the 41-year-old Vodicka is set to testify about how he had to put away his green uniform after breaking what he calls the cardinal rule of guards: Keep quiet in the face of officer brutality and corruption.

In a lawsuit filed against the state, Vodicka alleges that he blew the whistle on a gang of officers known as the "Green Wall" at Salinas Valley State Prison and was the subject of retaliation by co-workers and superior officers. The lawsuit contends that the Department of Corrections failed to shield Vodicka under the State's Whistleblower Protection Act. The Department, citing the lawsuit, declined to comment.

As I looked around the room my eyes met the faces of people I had worked with over the years—the people who refused to support me when it mattered. The idea of testifying in front of them, most of them senior to me in the chain of command, not to mention the senators and all the cameras, terrified me. I have always been a loyal, by-the-book kind of officer, respectful of the chain of command. To expose my profession's dirty laundry in public offended me.

Television networks would carry my hearing into every prison in the California system, everyone I had ever worked with would be watching. I knew from experience that the prison family paid close attention to news about itself. I would certainly be labeled "Snitch Vodicka".

I waited nervously to testify. For sixteen years, I tried to bring order and enforce the law in places where lawless chaos came naturally to the residents. I been proud of my job and believed I was good at it, with a file full of recommendations to support that belief. I didn't understand how I came to this point, getting ready to testify against my old partners, my peers, my fellow officers, my friends.

I stared at the empty witness chair; the room packed with eager spectators waiting to hear what I had to say. How could they possibly begin to understand my story? To understand The Green Wall you needed to know what prisons were really like and that took years of experience to learn.

"You okay there, partner?" asked Joe.

I was breathing fast, stressing out. I wasn't ready for this.

"Just tell them the truth, that's all you got to do. It's that simple."

Four hundred pairs of eyes fixated on me as my name was called by the bailiff.

"Donald Vodicka."

"Come on," said Lanny, "We're up."

I stepped through the low gate into the well of the Burton Room. I looked up at the bailiff.

"Raise your right hand," he ordered.

I raised my hand.

"Do you solemnly swear or affirm that the testimony you will give today before this committee will be the truth, the whole truth, and nothing but the truth?"

"I do."

Chapter Two

The Rookie

As part of its rapid expansion and new, highly acclaimed status, the Department of Corrections opened a training academy in Galt, in the San Joaquin Valley, in 1987. I entered with its third class in the spring of 1988. For the first time, guards were given badges, real uniforms, and professional training. The old-timers still called themselves prison guards, but the department and the union began pushing the title "Correctional Officer". Thus, the line between old school and new school was pretty clear.

For someone with military experience like I had, the academy was a piece of cake. Trainees lived in dorms, marched a lot, and attended classes in criminal law, case law, evidence handling, report writing and ethics and policies. A "Code of Silence" was never discussed while I attended the academy. Thirty percent of the class dropped out before the end of the six week course.

Physical exercise was required along with passing meticulous weapons qualifications. At that time, the weapons that the Department of Corrections used were: Smith and Wesson (S&W) .38 revolver, 12 gauge shot gun and open-sight carbine called the Mini-14. We also had baton training using the PR-24 hard plastic baton. The instructors where made up of veteran sergeants from different prisons throughout the state.

The prisons meanwhile were becoming dangerously overcrowded. A policy of "double-celling" was instituted, in which two inmates were packed into tiny cells intended for one. The new living arrangement promptly spiked violence and suicide rates within the system. This was called a temporary measure until new prisons could be built.

Don Novey, the former President of California's Correctional Officer's Union, was a special guest at my graduation; he gave a pep talk about the union and our responsibilities as correctional officers entering our new careers with the California Department of Corrections. My family came up for the graduation ceremonies. My mother pinned my badge, number *35121*, on my uniform shirt. It was the beginning of my dream career as a law enforcement officer.

In 1988, Corcoran State Prison opened as the largest prison in the nation, with a new architectural design to house the most dangerous inmates. Still empty when I arrived, I spent my first ninety days in a main gun tower.

I remember I was stationed alone in Gun Tower 6, a forty-foot high, sheet metal turret equipped with a sink, a toilet, a chair, combination intercom, shortwave radio, 12-gauge shotgun, Mini-14 carbine, and no air conditioner. There were twelve such towers spaced a hundred yards apart around the octagon-shaped perimeter of Corcoran State Prison. Inside each was a fellow rookie correctional officer, all recent graduates of the California Department of Corrections new training academy.

The new state prison in the town of Corcoran was the biggest local development since irrigation. When fully staffed and imprisoning the three thousand inmates it was designed for, it would be the largest, most expensive state-of-the-art prison in the world. In June of that year it was still empty, so the all-night watch was rookie duty, guarding a vacant prison.

There were two kinds of prisoners arriving at Corcoran that first summer. One group consisted of old-cons that'd been in the system for years. They came mostly from San Quentin or Folsom, the state's traditional felony prisons and asked to be transferred because it bumped them to the front of the line for programs. In the 1980's, American prisons still made an effort to rehabilitate criminals, offering vocational and educational programs that would better prepare them for life on the outside. In California, they earned double-time credit for enrolling in these programs; however massive overcrowding meant too few openings in coveted workshops and classes. By moving to a brand new prison they improved their chances of getting the cushy assignments that everyone wanted. Old-cons were patient, clever, ingratiating hustlers who long ago made a cliché of themselves.

The other early arrivals were involuntary transfers, repeat troublemakers that the state's fifteen other prisons wanted to be rid of, the bad-asses. They were usually younger than the old-cons, often ganged-up, men with too much anger or testosterone to get along in the close confines of prison. They had short tempers and attitude problems; many had mental or emotional issues and whenever a new prison opened, they were shipped from all across California to inaugurate it. Bad-asses were the main reason activating a prison was considered hardship duty by the California Department of Corrections (CDC)—worth the extra pay to the veteran guards who had agreed to do it.

Eventually there were middle ground inmates between those two extremes, but those early busloads had no room to spare for moderate characters. The department's green buses held thirty-four shackled prisoners and every day starting in June, three or four buses drove through the vehicle entrance to Corcoran's receiving area. Each had to stop between the fences atop a railed pit like those in industrial garages so the underside could be inspected. The bus guards got off to check their weapons in the gunroom. Then the interior gate was opened, the bus pulled forward and the men inside were unchained and disembarked, very cautiously. After long drives the bad-asses frequently emerged a little rowdy.

The southern end of the prison was divided into three main yards separated by tall razor-wire fences. Each yard had five cellblocks designed to house two hundred men. The prison's northern end was designed to contain the revolutionary "total control unit". That July, I drew third watch yard officer, scheduled from two o'clock in the afternoon to ten o'clock at night. The post and the shift were regarded as the most hazardous available—which both excited and terrified me.

The yards in California prisons are about the size of football fields, with weedy softball diamonds, cement basketball courts, concrete picnic tables, makeshift weight stands, and various other low quality amenities. Surrounding this sad amusement park were the gray-painted cinderblock walls of the housing units. Anywhere from two hundred to three hundred inmates can be on the yard at any one time, the number peaking in late afternoon when shops and classes shut down. Strolling among these proven criminals was a pair of wary guards armed with nothing more dangerous than a PR-24 hard plastic baton and a can of pepper spray. Our job was to act like we were in charge.

I can remember the night before my first day as a yard officer, out of the tower, on the ground amongst the inmates. I couldn't sleep. I kept going over in my mind all the warnings I'd been given by academy instructors about dealing with inmates:

> *"Don't tell them anything about yourself. Don't wear your wedding ring; don't talk about your girlfriend or your kids, what kind of car you drive, where you live, nothing personal. They've got friends on the outside. They'll remember you for years. They've got nothing to do but watch you. They can read lips. They'll never let up if you look like a victim. Never show fear."*

In the morning I unwrapped my brand new Class B greens so I'd look the best. The shirt was straw-colored with the departmental patch on the shoulder.

The twill pants were olive—not drab olive like the U.S. Army, but lush olive with a gold stripe down the seam. In my shirt pocket I placed two gold pens that matched the pant's stripe exactly. I pinned on my badge, CDC # 35121, my most proud possession.

Lastly, I tried on my favorite piece of equipment, the two-inch, black leather tactical utility belt I had ordered from the *Galls* catalogue, the nation's leading supplier of cop gear. It had custom pouches for handcuffs, gloves, pepper spray canisters, a notebook, and straps to hold a baton and a radio. It also had a smooth detachable sidearm holster for when I was outside the walls and wanted to carry. The belt was heavy, sturdy, and manly; it made me feel strong and ready when I buckled it on. I looked at myself in the mirror and shimmied a little, just to feel its weight shift around me.

The confidence it gave me had largely worn off by the time I reached the Yard A Program Office to relieve the second watch. I was handed a little Motorola radio with the red emergency button; my lifeline to backup.

There are few things more intimidating than walking onto a prison yard for the first time. In California prisons, a rookie guard and a newbie inmate are called the same, a "fish"—bait in the shark tank, food for the predators, chum. The natural defense for both kinds of fish was to try and look tough, puff out the chest and swagger a bit, stare back at everyone as coldly as possible, expressionless and hard. It's a ludicrous pose for most men under any circumstance and nowhere more ridiculous than in the middle of a maximum security prison yard. I was so taken aback by the first inmate who laughed at me that twenty years later I can still remember the man's name.

Because he is currently still in prison, I'll keep his identity private and call him Marvin Lloyd. If other inmates ever found out he had developed a respectful relationship with me, a guard, he would pay dearly. Marvin was tall, wiry, and middle-aged, with trashy tattoos and a redneck manner. He wore prison blues—the denim pants and shirt and rubber-soled shoes that were all manufactured in California prison workshops in those days. Stenciled on his shirt was a *B* inmate letter indicating he'd been inside for years already. He was an old-con who smoked hand-rolled cigarettes.

I was walking around like the meanest dude on the whole damn yard and thought I was pulling it off. After all, I was twenty-six years old, in prime condition, tall and jacked with Army muscle. I'd spent two hours driving iron at the gym that morning to get ready for my first day.

Marvin Lloyd took one look at me and burst out laughing.

"You're a fish!" He cackled loudly, pointing a bony finger at me like I was the most hilarious thing he'd ever seen.

I was stunned. My jaw fell open and I gaped at the scrawny redneck that couldn't stop laughing at me. Then I recovered and reacted the way I'd been trained, "Up against the wall, asshole."

Yard officers had a quota, every shift they were supposed to brace five or six inmates—put them against the wall and pat them down for contraband or weapons. At the academy we had practiced on each other dozens of times, it was drummed into us as a basic method of demonstrating who was in charge. This loud mouth was the first real inmate I had to pat down.

Marvin Lloyd had been braced by experts hundreds of times and wasn't impressed. He never stopped laughing as I patted him down. Not sure how rough to get, but pissed about being laughed at, I ordered gruffly, "Pull out your pockets."

The man knew the drill, pulled out empty pockets. "I got nothing boss," he chuckled.

"What's so damn funny?"

The chuckle subsided to a smile, "Nothing. Just makes me happy to see you, that's all."

My second day on the yard I responded to my first Code 3 alarm. As the siren blared, five hundred inmates smiled and got down on the ground. I yanked out my baton and looked around frantically for the source of trouble. Above the door on Building 3 was a flashing red light. I tucked the baton under my arm and took off running, dodging around prone-lying inmates like the hazards and obstacles they were. Half-a-dozen other officers were running for the same door, but I slammed through first. I sprinted down the narrow entry corridor and slammed through another door into the cellblock itself, inadvertently running right into the trouble.

The two floor officers already there—rookies like me—stood at a cell door screaming. "Stop! Get down on the floor!"

I hustled over for a look but the smell reached me before I got there, a stew of blood, vomit, and another stench I couldn't identify. Every cell had two windows of thick glass, one in the steel door and one to the side embedded in the concrete wall. Inside I saw two drunken skinheads trying to kill each other. The taller one had a weighted sock he swung at his shorter cellmate, who stabbed back viciously with a pencil. Both snarled and attacked with lunatic intensity, clubbing and stabbing at heads and eyes, neither aware of their own wounds and injuries. Their t-shirts and boxer shorts were drenched in blood, barf and some bright orange liquid. The only thing keeping them on their feet was inebriated fury.

I joined the floor officers in hollering at them to get down, but that was all we could do. Only sergeants and those ranked higher were authorized to open cell doors and a long minute passed before one of them came chugging up. The sergeant opened the door and emptied a canister of pepper spray into the cell while yelling at the maniacs, "Get down on the floor, now!"

Choking and gagging, the shorter skinhead dropped to his hands and knees. The tall one, however, kept wailing on his enemy with the heavy sack—a sock filled with soap bars—despite being blinded by the spray. The sergeant reached for his taser. He aimed carefully through the three-inch food port and shouted, "If you're not on the floor in two seconds I'm going to zap you!"

The warning was ignored and the sergeant fired. *Pop!* The tiny darts hit the still-fighting skinhead square in the chest and three hundred kilovolts bolted down the wire to transform him into jelly—quivering upright for the shock's four-second duration and then abruptly collapsing.

When the guards opened the cell it made everyone gag. There was blood, puke, piss, smeared shit, and pieces of flesh everywhere, even on the ceiling. The explosion of violence that had taken place in the small concrete box was extraordinary. None of the rookies had ever seen anything like it. I pinched my nose against the stench and stared in horrified wonderment. The med techs moved in promptly to start patching up the fighters. Miraculously, both were on their feet within minutes, still too drunk to feel any pain. The floor officers put them in handcuffs and leg restraints to prevent any further insanity and led them out of the cell. As they made their exit, other inmates gave them a hearty round of applause from their cells for the entertainment they had provided.

I was delegated to escort the shorter skinhead to Administrative Segregation (Ad/Seg)—the cellblock reserved for prisoners who needed to be isolated for any reason. The two men had been transferred together from Mule Creek Prison—a pair of bad-asses the officials there were pleased to unload on the new Corcoran facility. While neither was a known gang member, both sported white supremacist tattoos, had multiple convictions for assault and auto theft. They were as compatible as two hateful losers could be; they had volunteered to cell together.

Somehow they'd gotten their hands on some oranges and sugar and fermented a big jug of *pruno*, the beverage that prisons made famous. As generally sickening as it is alcoholic, pruno is simple to make and agreeably mind-bending like grain alcohol. The two men had gotten hammered and discovered a mutual loathing for each other. A fight to the finish was called for. They would both spend months in solitary confinement and have years tacked onto their already lengthy sentences as a consequence.

In my second week as a yard officer, I felt I was getting the hang of it; I wasn't so nervous anymore and the inmates no longer intimidated me. I stayed alert and cautious at all times. Knowing something, someone, could explode at any minute kept me on the edge. I wondered what Lloyd was in for and for how much longer, but fish guards didn't have access to inmate records and I couldn't just ask him. Asking or answering personal questions turned relationships personal and that was a bad idea. There were all kinds of rules against it and besides that—it felt weird. Although we developed a mutual liking for each other, I didn't want to be Lloyd's buddy. The old-con for his part was just angling for favoritism, not friendship. In a couple more weeks he was tipping me off to which inmates were selling drugs.

I realized pretty quickly that the academy had schooled me on departmental policies but didn't prepare me for the constant tension amongst inmates on the yard. It was a giant testosterone promenade, everyone flexing, strutting, showing off, and trying to assert their authority. There were relatively few fish inmates at Corcoran that first summer, so these were seasoned prisoners who knew more about the system than most of the guards—over half of them rookies like myself—and understood all the unwritten rules. I watched them and began to learn what school couldn't teach me.

The gangs were a revelation. I grew up in a middle class home in a small town so idyllic it made Mayberry seems sordid—I'd never even saw graffiti. The academy taught me the history of prison gangs and how to identify gang members, but watching them in action was a foreboding lesson. In 1988, gang membership wasn't yet illegal in America—not just cause for removal from the general population of a California prison—so the gangsters at Corcoran were fairly obvious. They flaunted gang tattoos, greeted each other with complicated handshakes, and occupied terrain like marine platoons—surrounding their chosen picnic tables with scowling sentries. It was a new yard in a new prison so control was up for grabs, and all the gangs wanted a piece.

In dominance games, the opening moves would be unfamiliar to outsiders. Sitting at the wrong picnic table, for instance, was an aggressive act. One of the gangs might claim the basketball court for itself one day, so another would counter by claiming it the next day, escalating the battle for dominance. It could also start in a cellblock, playing music too loud, changing the dayroom TV channel, or taking too long in the shower. Cutting in line at the chow-hall, flashing gang signs, or staring too hard were all provocations that demand a response in the world of prison gangs. It could be something as mundane as one gangster swiping another's dessert, which in fact, triggered the first riot at Corcoran.

Inmates were allowed to be out in the yard after the evening meal, from six thirty to eight thirty and before the nine o'clock count in their cells. In the cool air it was usually the most relaxed period of the day, although as boisterous and noisy as a grade school playground. On this one night, however, they emerged from the dining hall like funeral mourners—downcast and silent. The contending gangs moved in mass to their respective tables and posted lookouts all around. Anyone who wasn't involved slunk to the wall and sat down, making it clear they were non-combatants. This included every white or Asian man on the yard and half the Hispanics and blacks.

The guards didn't need a drum roll to tell them something serious was about to go down. The yard officers retreated to the Program Office, where Sergeant Marshall came out to see for himself. He called the watch commander to alert him, then the control booth officers in each of the five cellblocks, who sent gunners to the five roofs. The gunner in the yard tower aimed his rifle out the window. A floor officer from each unit stepped outside with an MK-9, which was a canister shaped like a fire extinguisher that could shoot a jet of pepper foam thirty feet. Old-time guards called it, "the big momma."

The opposing gangs saw these preparations but were unmoved. They'd been preparing for this all month and were ready to get it on. It was the Southern Hispanics, also known as the Mexican Mafia, against a provisional black alliance of the two gangs, Crips and Bloods. This alliance *never* existed before, as they themselves were enemies, and wouldn't last beyond this battle. Supremacy on the yard was at stake and nothing prison officials could do would have any affect on the outcome. The two sides were so focused on each other they attacked simultaneously, as if they heard a bell only gangsters could hear. Like nineteenth century warriors, they charged wildly across the yard, bellowing and brandishing weapons they'd been hiding for weeks—stuffed up their rectums, buried in the yard, or hidden in cells.

It was against department policy to let them fight but there weren't any policy-makers on hand just then.

"Stay right here," Sergeant Marshall told us. "I want you all to go home in one piece tonight. If they want to kill each other there's nothing we can do about it."

I couldn't believe what I was watching. Three hundred men collided violently in a massive, mindless, howling brawl. It was the most stupendously insane event I'd ever witnessed. I was so astonished I wasn't even scared to be standing there—at first.

"Yard down," boomed across the loudspeaker. "Yard down now!" It was Lieutenant Vella in the central control booth just ten feet above and behind where I stood with Sergeant Marshall and half-a-dozen other officers. "Yard down!"

The brawlers on the yard paid no attention, stabbing, kicking, and pummeling each other with mad abandon.

"Gunners," said Vella, now on the radio that only the guards could hear, "fire non-lethal rounds!"

Each gunner had a 37mm gas gun that could fire either tear gas grenades or wooden bullets, sized like hockey pucks. Non-lethal rounds were the hockey pucks, which academy trainees were taught to "skip" into the target instead of hitting it directly. They could cause significant injury if the target was a person, but again, this was a policy with limited meaning in the heat of a three hundred-man, insane riot. The gunners opened up—*pok-pok-pok-pok-pok*—the wooden bullets hit crazed men who yelped and jumped but didn't stop rioting for a second.

"Gunners, cease fire," said Vella after it was apparent that non-lethal rounds weren't working. "Floor officers, give them the gas. Don't stop until you're empty."

The five guards with the MK-9s moved into range and started hosing the melee. The foam jets had an orange tint and looked like the mightiest streams of piss since dinosaur days. Arcing in from five directions it soaked the rioters in concentrated chili juice—Oleoresin Capsicum, the active ingredient of pepper spray. Hard men cried out and fell to the ground, choking and gasping, heaving up their dinners. Other men though, kept stabbing, kicking, and pummeling blindly; only driven madder by the blistering agent.

A peppery-cloud spread across the yard and touched everyone, including the guards who—in 1988, in California—were not yet provided gas masks by their government employers. I felt it first in my eyes, which began to water and then sting like hell. My skin burned and my throat constricted, I coughed uncontrollably. I was getting scared now.

"Floor officers, fall back," instructed Vella on the radio. Then, on the loudspeaker he called out, "Gunners, lock and load live rounds. Stand by for lethal force."

The yard suddenly became very quiet. I could hardly see anything, but I heard the gunner on the roof above me rack the slide on his Mini-14 carbine. The bolts shot closed on six rifles overlooking the yard, and the snug clicks were quite distinct in the misty orange silence. My knees were shaking I was so scared.

"Down on the yard," yelled Vella loud and stern. "Now, or we start shooting!"

The last standing gangsters began to lie down. Most were Hispanic, the victors of the brawl—champions of the yard. It was a criminal triumph in every sense, meaningless outside the prison walls; an exercise in violence only gangsters could think was important.

"Yard officers, move out." said Vella. "Secure the yard."

Sergeant Marshall produced a sack full of plastic tie cuffs. I grabbed a handful and moved forward, wheezing, and hacking, blinking back tears. The hundreds of men on the ground were in worse condition, many of them bleeding from wounds or blunt force injuries—all dripping with stinging orange foam. There was little resistance as the guards moved among them, snapping on cuffs.

When the med techs hustled in with water hoses to rinse off the foam, they were hailed as saints by guards and gangsters alike.

The riot had lasted no more than ten minutes, but it took all night to clear the yard. The first watch relief arrived in time to collect weapons and help sort bad guys from bystanders; escort the former to Ad/Seg or the hospital and the latter to their cells. The yard was littered with makeshift knives and clubs, called inmate manufactured weapons. I got my first look at the Corcoran Investigative Services Unit when they showed up, the ISU Squad. They were called in from home to investigate and document the cause of the riot. Formal charges would be pressed against the instigators if they could be identified, sending them off to solitary and segregated housing for years to come. It was ISU that learned about the stolen scoop of ice cream that triggered the evening's madness.

When I trudged out to the parking lot at three in the morning, my eyes were still raw and red from the pepper gas and my nose wouldn't stop running. I was totally exhausted, but oddly exhilarated. For any kind of prison officer, but especially for a yard officer, that first big prison riot is a test and passage with real significance. I felt differently about myself now than I had two weeks ago, or even this morning. I took off my utility belt and laid it carefully in the trunk, then drove to my apartment for a couple hours sleep before coming back to work.

CHAPTER THREE

GANG LAND

Kody Scott was the same age as me that summer, twenty-six years old, but had come to prison by a far different path. When he was eleven years old, the night after graduating from elementary school, Kody was jumped into the neighborhood Crips gang after unloading all eight shots in a 12-gauge pump at some Bloods hanging on the wrong street; his teenage mentors had told him he couldn't come back to the car until the gun was empty. He earned his gang moniker at thirteen years old, after stomping a robbery victim so viciously it put the man in a coma. The police said only a monster could have done it. By sixteen, *Monster Kody* was a bicycle-pedaling terror, hyped on PCP, blasting away one-handed with a six-pound automatic he hardly bothered to aim. During one incident that year, he was himself shot six times at close range, cementing his reputation as a "Ghetto Star" by surviving somehow. At twenty years old, he was the brazen leader of the Eight Tray Gangster Crips, one of the most feared sets in the Balkanized-war zone of South Central Los Angeles.

In the summer of 1988, Scott was nearing his release date at Folsom Prison after doing four-and-a-half years on a seven-year sentence for two counts of attempted murder. This wasn't the famously gothic, century-old Folsom Prison where Johnny Cash recorded his classic album twenty years earlier, but a brand new maximum security facility erected next door and officially named, Sacramento State Prison. Everyone who worked or was incarcerated there still called it Folsom Prison or grudgingly, New Folsom. Like many other inmates, Scott found escape in reading while he was there, inspiring him to try his hand at writing. After his release he published *Monster: the Autobiography of an L.A. Gang Member*, in which he recorded his unruly journey through the California prison system. For instance:

> There were 13 of us CCO [Consolidated Crip Organization] in Soledad. I was in charge of C-wing. It was my duty to make sure that no Crips came out on the tiers with shower thongs on, because this was a security risk. One couldn't very well defend himself in shower shoes. I had to make sure that there were at least two knives out on the tier and available whenever we were out in the wing or the dayroom. I designated two people to carry the weapons. Any time one of us took a shower the area was cordoned off and secured. A quiet period was designated from 11:00 p.m. till 7:00 a.m. Every Saturday was mass exercise day. All 212Crips would form three huge circles on the yard and go through the routine.

The Crips weren't the only gang imbedded and organized within the general population of state prisoners. Another reformed gangster named "Huerito" Gratton, one of California's highest ranking prison gang members, also produced a book detailing his prison adventures. The Nuestra Familia, also known as Nuestra Raza or the Northern Structure, was a gang born in the late 1960's among inmates from the northern two-thirds of California, who felt themselves oppressed by the L.A-based Mexican Mafia. After twenty years, the Nuestra Familia had a brutal presence in every city from central California to Oregon by the time young Huerito took his first fall for dope-dealing. He arrived at Corcoran while I was there still learning the ropes.

Once at Corcoran, Gratton's orders were to report to the authority in charge, inform the leadership of his Nuestra Raza status and function hand-in-hand with all other NR and NF members at the facility. This was a common practice enforced and adhered to by all Nuestra Raza members, transferred from one facility to another.

After being given a firsthand tour of the prison, Gratton was assigned to function under the authority and/or guidance of Joseph "Jojo" Moreno, an extremely dangerous, well-known and respected NF member from Stockton, who was also second in command of overall security. Gratton was given a copy of Nuestra Raza's rules and regulations, known as the "14 Bonds". He was explained what was expected of him and his responsibilities, one of which was to memorize both the 14 Bonds and the NR Format.

Inmate Gratton spent the next couple of days studying the 14 Bonds and the NR Format and being introduced to numerous NR and NF members on the yard. He was impressed with their sophistication, knowledge, and know-how. Most of these gangsters had intellectual stature. Gratton, with no idea of the amount of time, effort, and energy these northern California prison gangs put into educating their members, decided to make his own education a priority.

Huerito soon discovered first hand the importance of his training. One morning, three weeks after Gratton's arrival at Corcoran State Prison, Sheldon "Skip" Villanueva called for all NF and NR members to gather at the handball courts for an emergency meeting. Once on the courts, all regimental members were advised that one of their allies, a Border Brother (BB) from Merced, had caught wind that Surenos were planning an attack and targeting any and all Nortenos during the next day's Cinco de Mayo festivities. Nortenos, who were outnumbered seven-to-one, decided to make a preemptive strike. Plans were made, targets set, and weapons were supplied. A few hours later, all hell broke loose when about twenty Nortenos went into the C Facility gymnasium and attacked a large group of unsuspecting Surenos.

I responded to the alarms and as soon as I got to the gymnasium door I observed several Hispanic inmates swinging wooden mop handles at any Mexican they saw in the line of sight. I stepped over one inmate that was knocked out on the floor. He had a huge chunk of skin missing on his forehead—he was bleeding profusely. There were puddles of blood on the floor and blood splashed across the walls. I heard screaming by inmates that where still conscious to feel their pain. The gymnasium was filled with pepper spray. Still without masks, my eyes burned. One inmate had a shank stuck in his left thigh and screamed in pain as two officers escorted him out of the gym to the medical clinic. We recovered several inmate manufactured stabbing weapons, such as a razor blade that was melted on a toothbrush—used as a slashing weapon. We also found soap bars inside of socks and tied in a knot, causing it to be a "sap" or a bludgeoning weapon. We also found several ice pick weapons with a white cloth handle.

To a young, fish yard officer barely five months out of the CDC Academy, most of this gang activity was invisible but menacing—a constant anxiety. They were the hidden movers of prison life, conspiring with and against each other to subvert the law and its institutions—especially the one they lived in.

The official policy of the Department of Corrections at that time, formulated by elected officials and administrators, was that every housing unit in every facility be integrated without regard to race or gang affiliation. The rationale for this policy was that men who were mortal enemies in their communities could become friends in prison, or at least accept each other's viewpoints. This no doubt sounded good in Sacramento. To the line guards in charge of implementing the fantasy, however, it was absurd, bloody, and the main reason prisons became uncontrollable.

August of 1988 saw the release of *Straight Outta Compton*, the double-platinum record sensation by N.W.A that launched "gangsta rap" into mainstream pop culture; without ever playing on the radio. The album's definitive song was *Fuck tha Police* and that attitude found its way into prison just as swiftly as balloon pants and bling appeared on MTV. Gangsters sent to maximum security, however, weren't celebrity posers but hard-core bangers who were proud to be there—it confirmed their gangster creed. They were expected to represent while inside.

I knew about the gangs. I knew they had dozens or hundreds of soldiers prepared to get it on, but often they were indistinguishable from the other miscreants and felons who populated Corcoran. In the 1980's, gang colors were still permitted—Crips and Nortenos wore blue rags in their pockets or Converse sneakers with the small blue star. Bloods and the Eme did the same in red but only "jumped in" members were allowed by the gangs to do so. Inmates, who weren't ganged up, quickly realized that independence made them vulnerable—easy marks for shakedowns and worse. They often hung out with hometown crews to pass as bangers, which made it even harder for an officer to know who was who amongst the members. Almost anyone could be a gangster. Breaking up groups of more than four men was the only way to ensure disruption of gang plans and prevent mass actions. For guards, this was an endless task.

"Alright, break it up, you know the rules," I would say to a bunch of five or six men walking together.

They'd make a show of splitting up until I spotted another pack across the yard and headed off to separate them. Then again, the first bunch would reassemble as if I had never reprimanded them. Sometimes groups would gather and break up repeatedly, alternating so the guards ping-ponged around to deal with them. The only way to stop this game was to brace the players, make them strip and submit to a rude search—which reliably took the fun out of anything.

I learned that tension on the yard could be gauged by the rise and fall of smack talk and face-offs, the macho theatrics of gang diplomacy. My first big riot had taught me that a yard on the verge of erupting was eerily calm— paused long enough for all the inmates to find their places. Less riotous but still ugly incidents were foretold by fewer obvious indicators—hushed words and slow concerted movements as the grapevine branched across the yard. Inmates sensed gang trouble the way herds of prey knew predators were circling. Watching them closely alerted a smart officer.

A peaceable yard was loud and vulgar, filled with anonymous criminals behaving randomly. Impromptu fist fights between angry prisoners were actually welcome diversions that released collective pressure, like gas flares in an oil refinery. Inmates whooped and hooted and I had the chance to take charge of the situation.

One day, I was watching some Crips play five-on-five basketball. As a former high school all-star and junior college scholarship player, I would get mesmerized watching good basketball, and some of these gangsters were really good. I was taken aback by the hard fouls and harder falls on the rough cement. The bangers would stop and scream raunchy curses at each other when fouls occurred, offending my sense of hoops decorum.

A willowy player named Robinson went in for a layup and another Crip, a stocky weightlifter named Hester, yanked his legs out from under him and Robinson crashed painfully to the ground. He got up quickly and was in Hester's face, both yelling "motherfucker" at the top of their lungs. Then the skinny one smashed the weightlifter's nose and the fight was on. I ran forward to break it up but every inmate in the area was rushing in to cheer and holler at the same time. I radioed the gun tower to sound the alarm and put down the yard. The surrounding inmates followed orders, laid prone on the ground allowing me to stop the fight and cuff the two fighters.

Normally they'd go to Ad/Seg for several months and have a year or two added to their sentences for assault. In this case though, the yard's Crip shot-caller intervened. Convicted murderer Kerwin "Payback" Holcomb was an "original gangster" from the Rolling Sixties, a legendary Crip set. He was a tall, lanky man with a Rick James hair-do who usually had an entourage of five or six buff thugs to protect him. He, however, walked by himself into Lieutenant Vella's office. He told Vella that the fight disrespected the game of basketball and the Crips were sorry for it. He said he would make sure it didn't happen again if Vella cut his boys some slack. Robinson and Hester got two weeks in Ad/Seg and had to sign waivers absolving the Department of Corrections of responsibility if they hurt one another in the future.

The incident also began a relationship between me and Inmate Hester. The Bakersfield Crip had an easy laugh and joking manner that never failed to crack me up. Inmate Hester had grown up in a broken home with a welfare mom—a world apart from my stable, middle-class boyhood. Hester's stories of childhood poverty and juvenile delinquency—told with the panache of a natural born comedian—were illuminating as well as funny. I was too much of a cop to ever sympathize with law-breaking, but it made me less judgmental about my prisoners.

Hester was also a diligent worker, so I got him assigned to work crews that he would supervise. This had advantages for both us, the kind of prison partnership that eases life inside the walls. Working together on a regular basis had a normalcy about it that helped pass the time and improve the work, meeting the needs of both prisoner and guard. Years later, after I moved on to other prisons and Hester made parole, another Crip told me that David Hester had been killed in a car chase with police. To my surprise, I felt saddened when I heard the news.

I loved being a yard officer. It put me closer to the inmates than any other posting available to a fish guard. It was also the most dangerous job for the same reason, but that was okay with me. There were plenty of veteran correctional officers who couldn't handle yard duty, lurking near the program office their entire shift and allowing the place to police itself—which meant gang rule. Doing yard duty in prison was like going Airborne in the Army; it offered a challenge and a rush that appealed to my gung-ho nature. It was special, only for the elite.

I took the kind of pride in my job that some of my peers would call arrogance, but as a young rookie it made me stand out. When my three-month tour was up, Lieutenant Vella and Sergeant Marshall both gave me the highest marks they could; they asked me to come back to A Yard after completing my probation. I happily accepted. By this time B and C yards had also filled up and Corcoran was nearing capacity, so quality yard officers were in demand.

When the new rookie assignments were posted I was disappointed. I was going to be a transportation officer in the main prison kitchen, which sounded to an Army vet an awful lot like kitchen patrol. I couldn't imagine I'd learn anything useful or advance my fledgling career by working in the kitchen. I was utterly wrong on both counts.

Chapter Four

Kitchen Cop

The biggest prison in the United States required a huge kitchen capable of turning out six thousand hot meals a day plus at least three thousand sack lunches. It was about as massive as an airplane hangar, with loading docks for shipping and receiving, dry and cold storage lockers, a butcher shop, bakery, prep rooms, industrial stoves, ovens and fry stations, and a giant scullery. All of which were partitioned by cinder block walls with lockable steel doors. It was poorly designed for a prison facility, modeled on large institutional kitchens where food was the priority instead of security. There were poor sight lines and long hallways with too many corners, and the guard station was stuck in an isolated corner. Over two hundred inmates worked in the kitchen and nearly all belonged to gangs. Each of the gangs had a specialty area: The Crips chopped vegetables, the Eme made sandwiches, the Aryan Brothers and Nazi Low Riders washed pots and pans and nobody got in anyone's face because they were kept apart. It was the only place at Corcoran where the integration rule was ignored.

For a prison inmate, a job in the kitchen was the next best thing to a millionaire cellmate. It meant eating better than anyone else, including the staff, and the other inmates all befriended them in hopes of sharing smuggled goodies. The most desirable goods were sugar, bread, and any kind of spoiled fruit that could ferment into execrable wine—the makings of serious pruno. Because the kitchen served all three yards, it was outside the fencing, although still inside the walls—which for the inmates brought a small taste of freedom going to and from work.

Supervising these two hundred prisoners were seven scared civilian food service professionals and four correctional officers led by Sergeant Charlie Martinez and Officer Joe Reynoso. Martinez was a stocky, barrel-chested, hard-ass veteran who scared other guards as much as the inmates. Reynoso was an eager up-and-comer who couldn't get enough of the job. He signed up for any and all extra training offered and volunteered for the SERT Squad, Special Emergency Response Team—the prison equivalent of SWAT. Martinez ran the place as he saw fit. Segregating the gangs was his idea, which he described to prison administrators as making sure his workers were "compatible." Since the kitchen was outside the yards, they were a long way from backup and Martinez figured if the honchos didn't like it they could suck on their pencils.

I showed up for work on first day in the kitchen as I had when I started on A yard—wearing my best Class B Uniform, spit-shined and polished from my boots to my badge. Sergeant Martinez glared at me as if he was personally offended.

"We don't dress up around here," said the gruff sergeant. "This is the kitchen, it's messy. Shit gets spilled on you. You see me all dressed up?"

Martinez was wearing the one-piece green CDC jumpsuit that sold for one hundred dollars at Corcoran's uniform store. I had never seen anyone wearing one on duty before.

"No, sergeant," I said meekly.

"You see anyone else around here all dressed up?"

I looked around. The only other officer in sight was Reynoso, who was wearing a jumpsuit too, "No, sergeant."

"Then get with the program, starting tomorrow. You hear me?"

I was so rattled I almost saluted, "Yes, sergeant!"

Reynoso stifled a laugh. A lean and wiry man, Reynoso was used to dealing with men much bigger than himself, but he'd never seen one so plainly embarrassed before. He liked me from the start because of it.

"Joe," said Martinez. "Why don't you show this kid what he's supposed to do? Make sure he doesn't fuck up too bad."

Reynoso got up and offered his hand. "Welcome to the kitchen," he said to me as I grasped his hand gratefully. "We run a pretty tight ship here."

As the two of us toured the mammoth kitchen, Reynoso told me their secret for running the ship.

"We get the biggest, meanest, most badass son-of-a-bitch we can find in each clique and make him lead man for that area. Clean-up, vegetables, whatever, it's his job to control his people. If there's any trouble, he's gone."

Prison jobs paid between ten and ninety cents an hour and were deposited directly into an inmate's prison account, the only money most of them had. Lead men got top wages. At each stop on the tour I was duly impressed by the size and intimidating persona of the area's chief gangster. I was troubled by Martinez's confidence in the prisoners. Kitchen workers handled some dangerous tools, from knives and cleavers to frying pans and steam guns.

Four guards armed with plastic batons wouldn't stand much of a chance if the inmates ever wanted to take over.

The Corcoran kitchen was my first big lesson in the necessary interdependence, the cruel partnership of prisoners and their guards. The place couldn't function without cooperation and that wouldn't happen without mutual respect for the other side's leaders and rules. If a lead man chose to fire someone on his crew, that was his decision and Martinez didn't question it. Men with fresh bruises sometimes stopped at his office to tell him they'd lost their jobs. As long as the work got done and no one got sent to the hospital he didn't interfere in gang business.

At the end of the tour, Reynoso and I reached the rear loading dock where my job awaited. The meals prepared in the kitchen were eaten in dining halls located in each of the three yards. They were ferried there by transport officers in a box truck holding nine large food carts with at least one hundred meals in each. The overnight shift got breakfast and bag lunches out to the yards. I would be making three trips to deliver dinner. There were inmate crews at both ends to help load and unload the carts, but it was my responsibility to make sure nothing was lost or spilled—or more likely stolen.

Reynoso waved forward a gigantic man with *Peckerwood* tattooed boldly on both enormous arms.

"This is Inmate Childress; he's your lead man. This is Officer Vodicka, the new transport officer."

We didn't shake hands because guards and prisoners never shook hands. Rather, we acknowledged one another with infinitesimal head nods and locked eyes for the briefest of moments; myself trying hard to look nonchalant.

Holy shit, I thought, *he's bigger than Arnold Schwarzenegger.*

Despite the "prison distance", we came to know each other well in the time to come. I would watch in awe as Childress—Inmate C-12345, forty-one years old from Modesto sentenced to thirty years for second degree murder—curled one hundred-pound dumbbells in each hand. He was imperturbable, soft spoken and called the shots for all the white gangsters on C yard.

The other five men in the back dock crew were all white supremacists who promptly did whatever Childress told them to do. They expertly loaded the truck while Reynoso and I climbed in the cab.

Before we were halfway through that first day's deliveries, the rookie and the veteran found they had much in common. We had both been high school star athletes, I in basketball, Reynoso in baseball. We both went on to play junior college ball, where we realized we weren't good enough to go pro. We both had dreamed of becoming policemen since we were boys and joined the Department of Corrections because it paid better and had openings. Neither one of us regretted the decision.

By the time we finished unloading at C yard, while the inmate crew stacked dirty breakfast trays in the truck, Reynoso turned to me and asked, "Do I have to call you Vodicka or can I use your first name?" It was the first time a senior officer had asked me that.

Within two weeks we were organizing the Corcoran Prison staff softball team and entering local tournaments. Reynoso was the sparkplug shortstop and I was the burly cleanup hitter. The team we led stomped everyone in town. Playing ball was fun and addicting, so we started making road trips around the Central Valley to play against fire stations, police departments, and company teams, basically anyone we could line up. An easy friendship grew out of the game.

In the kitchen though, I still got the rookie treatment. Whenever some thankless task needed doing it fell automatically to "fish Vodicka," assigned invariably with chuckles and grins from Charlie and Joe. The most tiresome errand was the lunch run. Prison staff didn't share kitchen food, which was for prisoners only. So I was dispatched daily to the staff cafeteria in the Administration Building, at the opposite end of the prison. Charlie and Joe gave me their orders and meal tickets as I trudged off to fill them—frequently paying from my pocket when the tickets didn't cover their appetites. I was so accommodating it invited abuse. In the usual way of male hazing rituals, the hazers pushed it until I stood my ground.

After several weeks of fetching burritos and cheeseburgers I finally declared, "I'm tired of getting lunch all the time. It's someone else's turn."

Charlie sat back in his chair with a shocked expression. "Oh-ho!" he exclaimed dramatically. "He's tired of getting lunch!"

For a long nervous moment I worried that I should have kept my mouth shut.

Then Joe stood up with an equally dramatic sigh. "Damn," he said, "I guess I can go today."

It wasn't long after that I started getting invited to watch weekend pay-per-view fights at the Martinez home in Visalia, where I met Charlie's wife and kids. It was then when I started to feel like I truly belonged. Like most law enforcement subcultures, correctional officers are insular, traditional and often related—Charlie's father-in-law was a twenty-year man, Joe's wife a probation officer. My first connection to this professional family came during those fight-night barbecues and marked the difference between having a job and a career.

It also saved my rookie ass when I screwed up. Once, I pushed the wrong button on the tailgate lift and dumped three hundred dinners on the B yard sidewalk. Charlie was so furious he made Joe leave the office while he ripped me a new one; but he didn't fire me. He even defended me when the civilian kitchen manager, Mr. Hart, wanted to fire me.

But my principal education in the Corcoran kitchen came from watching Martinez and Reynoso handle convicts. They had zero tolerance for disrespect; bracing inmates before the second syllable of "fuck you" was out of their mouths. They rarely swore or raised their voices when talking to a prisoner and always addressed them formally as "Inmate Smith" or "Inmate Ruiz." It was the same exaggerated courtesy that street cops use with citizens and it had the same effect—calming some and irritating others. The ones who got irritated generally didn't last long in the kitchen, but it wasn't the correctional officers who got rid of them. It was their leader, who observed the same etiquette. Respect was the currency of prison life and anyone who refused to pay it properly had a hard time getting along, whether they wore blue or green.

Martinez and Reynoso watched me just as closely as I watched them. The correctional family was suspicious and selective about accepting new lifetime members. The judgment of senior officers was crucial in winning promotions or good assignments. The standard they used was how the wannabes handled prisoners. They looked for people who understood the difference between displaying authority and demeaning an inmate, someone who demanded order and control and frankly, wasn't a born asshole.

This informal vetting still worked reasonably well in the early 1980's. The California prison system still enjoyed a nationwide reputation for innovation and rehabilitation that carried over from the glory days of the 1950's and 1960's— when the state was riding high and its institutions benefited. But those days were long gone by 1988. The prisons especially, were headed for disaster and the largest of them all would be in the forefront. America's approach to crime and punishment was changing radically and Corcoran was soon to become the poster prison for everything that could go fatally wrong.

I completed my probation by the end of 1988 and was scouting for a way to advance my new career. Like many of the young guards at Corcoran, I looked across the interior wall dividing the yards from the "total control facility" that was scheduled to open in early 1989. Formally called the Security Housing Unit (SHU), it represented the most significant development in prison management and architecture in decades, and ambitious correctional officers all wanted to be part of it. Two-thirds of the twelve hundred-person Corcoran staff put in for assignment there, only a hundred of whom would be needed.

Charlie Martinez thought he was doing me a favor when he asked me if I wanted to run the third watch shift in the SHU kitchen.

I told him, "It would be an honor to open the SHU Kitchen."

I lied. I was bored with the same drill everyday. I remember Captain Richard Giles, the SHU captain refused to consider another assignment for me, despite repeated requests. Wistfully, I had been watching the ISU Squad. Their uniform was an elite-looking midnight black, different from a line officer who wore a green jumpsuit. They had full access to the prison grounds, the authority to go anywhere they needed to go to enforce the law inside the prison walls. This was what I wanted to do.

Chapter Five

Famous Corcoran SHU

On the same day in October, 1983, two guards were killed in separate incidents at the US Penitentiary in Marion, Illinois. Opened ten years earlier as the replacement for Alcatraz,

FSP-Marion was built to house the most dangerous three hundred men in federal custody and was considered the most secure prison in the country. Neither murder was a spontaneous attack, both displayed planning and conspiracy amongst several inmates. The victims however, were matters of chance, whichever guard was on duty at the time would be killed. The response by prison authorities was to lock every prisoner in their cell for a little more than twenty-two hours a day with no visits or phone calls, no work or education programs, not even access to religious services. Taken out only to shower or exercise individually, they were isolated from the staff and each other as completely as the prison's design allowed them to be.

Prison lockdowns were a common and longstanding emergency measure that the courts had judged a reasonable response to any confusing or volatile situation, and prison wardens didn't hesitate to impose them. Lockdowns in old-fashioned prisons though, with the inmates all behind bars in neighboring cells on crowded tiers, resembled a vulgar production of *Jailhouse Rock*. They brought on such a stir-crazy racket that the guards would want everyone back on their normal schedule as quickly as possible, so lockdowns rarely lasted longer than a few days.

In modern day Marion however, the cells were concrete cubicles with solid steel doors that made isolation real and profound, closer to entombment than mere imprisonment. The locked down inmates had no human contact except for the guards who shackled them to go outside for their hour of lonely exercise. But what made the "Marion Lockdown" famous was that it went on for weeks and weeks, then months and months, and finally for years. It was solitary confinement so radical that psychologists studied it, scholarly papers were written about it and prison administrators around the world watched pensively as it continued on.

In the same year, 1983, the legislature passed five prodigal bond issues totaling more than 2.6 billion dollars to finance new prisons. It was California's grandest extravagance since irrigating the Central Valley in the 1940's or funding brilliant universities in the 1960's, and illustrated perfectly the direction in which things were going. The building boom was supervised by the Department of Corrections, the fastest growing agency in state government.

In 1987, a federal judge in Illinois dismissed the long-pending lawsuit filed on behalf of Marion inmates claiming that endless lockdown was unconstitutional. His opinion was upheld by the Fifth Circuit Court of Appeals, which called conditions in the prison "ghastly", "horrible" and "depressing in the extreme", but not cruel and unusual. The worrisome cloud of judicial review had been lifted from the dream of total control.

The need for control was the law's response to the growing menace of outlaw gangs, which all traced their lineage and authority back to felony prisons. Conventional maximum security had done nothing to isolate the gang lords from their foot soldiers; in fact it did just the reverse. Ambitious bangers regarded hard time as career advancement, a chance to get close to the boss.

> *"Prison was like a stepping stone to manhood. Your 'work' brought you in contact with the police and since jail was part of the job description, you simply prepared ahead of time for the mind-fuck of being a prisoner."*
>
> *-Monster Kody Scott*

The "mind-fuck" climax was in solitary, and a dedicated banger wanted to get there. Even after achieving a prison sentence and managing to get sent to a maximum security prison for flagrant gang-banging, it was still necessary to stomp someone. Preferably the target was a gang rival, but guards were acceptable—in order to reach the pinnacle of segregated housing, where the big dogs lived. A steady traffic of these climbers kept the gangs in business and the lawmen frustrated, unable to choke the flow of gangland information.

The Security Housing Unit at Corcoran was designed to contain 240 grisly men, like bugs in amber. By the time it opened in late January, 1989, however, the entire prison system was so overbooked that even solitary confinement had to be doubled up; each eight-by-eleven-foot cell had side by side cement platforms for beds with space underneath for personal items. At the rear, a cement shelf made a desk with a slit window above it offering a view of the nearby wall. Next to the desk was a one-piece extruded aluminum sink-toilet combo that had no sharp edges, knobs or accessible pipes and was bolted flush into the concrete floor. The floor, ceiling, and walls were painted drab gray. The door was perforated steel with 8,200 holes in it according to Monster Kody, who counted each of them while in solitary one day.

There were two floors of ten cells in a row with a shower cell in the middle. Two such wings constituted a *pod*. Both wings were angled to face the pod control booth so that inmates looking out their cell doors could see only a guard looking back at them; no other cells or humans were visible. There were three pods in each of four SHU buildings, but no prisoners yet when I arrived to stock the kitchen and checkout the equipment. I carried pots, ladles, and warming trays over myself because there weren't any inmate crews yet approved for the new, still secret, ultra-security unit.

Work crews for the SHU would come from C yard, the yard closest to the SHU compound, which is where I started interviewing applicants. I signed up inmates Hester and Childress, the Bakersfield Crip and the white supremacist, and old-con Lloyd from my first days on A yard. For my lead man I picked Inmate Gunter, a thirty-year-old surfer dude with the five-point star tattoo on his throat that Orange County criminals of all races favored. He had cooking experience both inside and outside of prison and a get-straight attitude that I wanted to encourage. I didn't know Gunter's first name or why he was in prison, but that was standard; I didn't know Hester's or Childress's first names or crimes either—and I'd worked with them for almost a year. Relationships between guards and prisoners were about as existential as they come, as constrained by walls and time as the space they occupied—immune to real-world curiosity.

Nearly half of the twenty-man crew I assembled was made up of Border Brothers, prison lingo for illegal Latin American nationals. In my mind they were highly reliable, the busboy backbone of every restaurant I'd ever been in. They stuck together and shared jobs to spread the meager pay among their compatriots, and I respected that. As long as one of them spoke kitchen-English I could make it work.

Each crew member needed picture ID to gain access to the SHU, even wearing restraints and under escort. Every afternoon when my shift began, I'd go to the C yard Program Office where they'd be waiting—I'd chain them up and sign them out, then march them fifty yards to the SHU gate where a pair of guards checked their ID's against a list. They'd all be unchained, stripped down for anal inspections, scanned head to toe with a metal detector, then re-dressed, re-chained, and marched another twenty yards to the SHU kitchen. It took an hour just to get everyone to the job site.

On the January afternoon when the first SHU prisoners were due to arrive, my crew and I were taking a break near the kitchen's rear loading dock.

We heard the first bus drive into the unit, coming from Old Folsom, where the state's top prison gang leaders had been doing time for years. Unlike general population inmates, SHU prisoners were unloaded in shackles and taken directly to their cells, no stopping at receiving for prints and photos and stern lectures; not an unguarded moment when they might cause trouble.

Even so, within minutes of the first bus pulling in, we heard the *pok-pok-pok* of gas guns firing wooden bullets. My crew and I went quiet at the sound. We then, saw and smelled the gun smoke wafting over the top of Building 1.

"Oh man," groaned inmate Hester, "that don't sound good."

"Sounds like open season over there," muttered inmate Lloyd.

There was another hail of *pok-pok-pok*, then a pause with more smoke, then *pok-pok-pok*. The Border Brothers looked strenuously at their feet in an effort to become invisible.

To me it sounded exciting. A mighty thrill rushed up my spine with the tingling awareness that I was close to the action, like a soldier nearing the front lines. It was more of a head trip than adrenaline rush, confirmation that I was in a serious place doing something significant—the sort of feedback young men crave and seem to get most definitively when guns are firing. I would have smiled if my inmate crew wasn't looking so glum.

I learned from my other coworkers that a fight had broken out. A small, no-name, white inmate got his head bounced into a wall so hard, that blood and brain matter was all over the concrete. He would have been killed if the smoke didn't stop the other inmates from beating him further.

During the next few weeks, buses arrived from the twenty-two other state prisons, empting their inmates convicted of major assaults, on me and my staff. Many were hardcore gang-bangers, but others were just hard cases—men who fought so readily they had to be isolated from the general run of tough guys on the yard. They had all been sentenced to solitary and most were used to it, but wherever they came from it wasn't nearly as harsh or restrictive as what greeted them at the Corcoran SHU.

Sacramento had designated it a pilot program, an experiment to discover the practical limits of total control. This meant, among other rules, that SHU prisoners were allowed only six cubic feet of personal items because that's all that would fit under the concrete beds in their new cells. There had been no such limit in their previous prisons and most arrived with too many boxes of personal belongings, which the Corcoran guards grinningly tape-measured and pronounced excessive. They could either ship it home at their own expense or donate it to oblivion; they had to decide right then and there at the bus stop. *Welcome to the SHU, pal.*

There were other new rules encountered that first day. SHU prisoners couldn't wear their own clothes or even prison blues, but instead were issued cheap, yellow rayon jumpsuits. Headquarters were thinking about phasing in these jumpsuits system-wide, since no gang had ever claimed yellow as their color. Similarly, the Converse All-Stars that bangers loved for their symbolic colors were replaced in the SHU with ugly, piss-colored sneakers that looked like duck's feet. Another new rule involved the personal television sets that many veteran convicts had lugged from cell to cell for years; the SHU required them to have clear plastic housings so nothing could be hidden inside among the wires and circuit boards. This meant just about every one of those beloved TVs were left behind in the parking lot, next to their favorite clothes, shoes, and excess baggage.

But the rudest shock of all was the "no tobacco" rule, the first of its kind at any prison in America. Now more than ever, snatching a man's cigarettes was a guaranteed fist fight. All in all, the new arrivals' first reaction to the place was to get mightily, self righteously pissed off, and the guards got used to it quickly. The gas guns were kept close at hand. It took about six weeks to fill three SHU buildings with top-rank gangsters and short-fused brawlers, all mixed together in keeping in accordance with official state policy. None of them liked their new home.

There were two small, high-walled exercise yards for SHU inmates, like concrete handball courts, where one pod tier at a time, fifteen or twenty angry men wearing boxers, t-shirts and flip-flops, were released for ninety minutes of daily mingling. They fought from the first day, either one-on-one or altogether, and they weren't wimpy slappers but brutal stompers who didn't back off when a man was down. The only way to stop the fighting was with wooden bullets fired by the gunner overlooking the scene.

There were no yard officers in the small SHU yards. Even in Sacramento, they knew that was a job too dangerous for anyone. Instead, there was a gunner in a second floor window who could see everything and issue firm orders—just like headquarters' policy-makers. Besides his wooden bullet gas gun, this gun post officer was armed with a Heckler & Koch 9mm assault rifle that fired Glaser blue tip 9mm rounds—the same weapon issued to most California police department SWAT teams. He was under instructions to use lethal force whenever he thought someone's life was threatened, whether guard or inmate. This would logically be a position for a veteran officer with proven judgment but that wasn't the case. There weren't enough veteran officers to go around in the rapidly expanding, undermanned and overcrowded prison system.

My job was more prosaic, but kept me busy. Feeding dinner in the SHU meant rounding up my crew by mid-afternoon, loading the precooked meals at the main kitchen, driving them through security with a cart-towing tractor to the SHU kitchen, then warming the food and serving it up on syrofoam trays that couldn't be made into sharp blades. The floor officers in each pod made the actual deliveries to the inmates in their cells through small ports in the perforated steel doors. My crew handled clean up and returned the warming trays to the main kitchen before I escorted inmates back to C yard; they were strip-searched and shackled again.

I had acquired a partner by this time, a spit-shined new-comer from Selma, California, named Jesse Gonzalez who graduated from the California Department of Corrections Academy two classes behind me. At first he was a junior partner and treated accordingly—with the same curt scrutiny that I had faced—but, it only took a few weeks for Officer Gonzalez to become Jesse. We both had a serious demeanor that revealed itself in attention to detail, from shiny pots to correct uniforms. It soon evolved into a got-your-back trust that cops always hope to find in their partners. The SHU kitchen was a smooth-running operation by early March; when the last SHU prisoners were due to arrive.

At Corcoran, one pod had been reserved for protective custody, the home for prisoners so treacherous or notorious they needed to be kept out of sight and sequestered from human consciousness—men like Sirhan Sirhan, Robert Kennedy's assassin, and Juan Corona, the "Machete Murderer" who hacked up twenty-five migrant workers in six weeks—averaging an all-time record of one murder every forty hours. Corcoran had a whole tier of serial killers; "Freeway Killers" William Brown and Patrick Kearney, who killed twenty boys each; "Hillside Strangler" Angelo Buono, who murdered ten women; and "Night Stalker" Ricardo Ramirez, a serial killer responsible for taking fourteen innocent lives. In fact, Corcoran imprisoned the first man ever tagged with the "serial killer" title, Edmund Kemper III. Called "The Coed Killer" when still at large in Santa Cruz, Kemper was the model for the "Buffalo Bill" character in the Thomas Harris novel, *The Silence of the Lambs*. After interviewing him in jail in 1972, FBI Agent Robert Ressler, founder of the agency's heralded Violent Criminal Apprehension Program (V.I.C.A.P), coined the term "serial killer" to describe Kemper's monstrous habit.

The atrocities these new inmates committed were beyond brutal, even for violent criminals, so they had to be segregated for their own protection. Their infamy made them targets for prisoners with nothing to lose; redemption to be won by striking at the first opportunity. They survived only by extraordinary exile to the most remote corners of state prisons, which is how they ended up in the Corcoran SHU. By the time they arrived here, Kemper and his fellow psychopaths were all pudgy and sallow from sedentary years spent recalling the horrors they inflicted. They even had the audacity to constantly whine for extra dinners.

The most infamous prisoner of them all arrived that month to take up residence. I was early to work that day and went for a stroll on the roof of Building 4, which looked out across broad cotton fields to the north and west. From a long ways off I could see a small convoy of green CDC vehicles—two SUV's escorting a van in the middle. The lead SUV was clearly in radio contact with the main security office because guards were waiting at every gate to wave them through without stopping; which I had never seen happen before.

The convoy pulled up right below me, where the Protective Housing Unit was located. Six correctional officers jumped from the SUV's brandishing rifles and shotguns to secure the area—like a Secret Service detail protecting the President. One of the officers looked up and saw me. I held up my hands to show I was harmless, but the officer still aimed his shotgun at me and ordered me away from the entrance. The team leader signaled to the van and the side door slid open. Two burly officers emerged, looked around, then reached inside and lifted out a small skinny man wrapped in chains; it was Charles Manson.

Like several other mass murderers who came to the SHU of Corcoran, Manson had escaped the gas chamber when the California Supreme Court overturned the death penalty in the early 70's. In another stroke of luck his notoriety preceded the 1982 state law, passed largely because of him, that prohibited criminals from profiting on their guilt. In San Quentin, he'd become rich selling autographs, drawings, bad poems, and songs to his fans. This made other prisoners envious, especially those who thought themselves more hardcore than some sick hippie baby-killer. Charles Manson was the number one target in the whole prison system and everybody knew it—including him. The first thing he did when he got to Corcoran was buy new SHU-approved TV sets for all the inmates in his pod.

Three weeks later, the first SHU inmate was shot to death. His name was William Martinez and he was a thirty-year-old Nuestra Familia gangster convicted of armed robbery in Oakland. He and Pedro Lomelli, an Eme member from Los Angeles, had been restricted to their cells for ten days for fighting. As soon as their restriction was over, on April 7th, they were right back at it. The security video shows Martinez charging across the yard at Lomelli the second he comes out the door.

The gun post officer was a smart, vaguely nerdy twenty-five-year-old named Robert "Rob" Christian who had been in my class at the academy. He'd been on the job for less than a year and was standing guard over the most hardened, angry gangsters in any prison in the country with orders to use lethal force if anyone's life was threatened. The video shows the two bangers wailing on each other for thirteen seconds before Lomelli goes down and Martinez, still in his flip-flops, starts kicking him violently. Wooden bullets were fired, but missed both fighters. At that point, Martinez steps back, but Christian was already busy with the H & K—chambering one of the Glazer safety rounds that were standard issue to police and prison guards because the blue Teflon tips shattered easily on impact minimizing the risk of ricochets when used in close quarters. They made a nasty big hole when they hit something soft however, like the middle of Martinez's back.

At the shooting review board, Christian testified that Martinez was kicking Lomelli in the head when he fired, and it probably did seem that way to him. A stopwatch on the video shows a four second pause between the last kick and the gunshot, but that's just a blink when a scared young man's adrenaline is racing.

The board backed him and called the shooting justified, establishing a precedent that other Corcoran review boards would follow time and again in the bloody months and years to come.

This incident made me realize I had options. Every prison in the state was shorthanded and experienced guards were needed in all of them. The state was paying moving expenses and per diem for sixty days until candidates found residency. At this point, I would have more seniority at a brand new prison. So when I saw the flyer from Sacramento seeking lateral transfers for Calipatria State Prison, a maximum state prison located in the lower desert of California, I submitted my transfer package request immediately and escaped the SHU kitchen.

CHAPTER SIX

NIGHT LIFE

Calipatria State Prison had issued me a reporting date of December 1, 1991. I saw the look on Sergeants Grandy's face; he was sad and disappointed that I was going to be transferring to a new institution. My kitchen partner and best friend Correctional Officer Jesse Gonzales gave me a big hug and said, "I will miss you, you son of a bitch. Who am I going to go out and party with?"

Jesse and I did a lot of partying together off duty. On my birthday that year, we headed off to Fresno, California to our favorite place, the bar in the airport Holiday Inn. Both being single, good-looking guys, we didn't have any problem meeting ladies to socialize with. It was happy hour and lined up in front of us were five Kamikaze shots which were followed by several Long Island Iced Teas.

Around nine o 'clock that night, Jesse and I headed to the Famous Black Angus Restaurant in downtown Fresno, where the Fresno State University college girls hung out. But before going to the Angus, we stopped at the place next door to it, another bar called Wilkers. Surprisingly, it had a four-to-one ratio, women to men.

Being the ladies man that he was, Jesse floated through the crowd chatting up the girls left and right. Me, being the more laid back kind of guy, stayed at the bar and just observed the crowd. Clustered of pretty girls were every three feet, the music was blaring, the drinks had started to hit me, and I had work in the morning. Suddenly, Jesse was gone—probably headed next door to the Angus looking for more ladies.

Sure enough, Jesse was at the Angus, on the dance floor with a gorgeous blond dancing up a storm. Once again, I found refuge by the bar. My people-watching was distracted by two Fresno police officers making their way towards the bar—towards me.

When they approached me, they asked me to step outside with them. Confused, I obeyed and once outside, I saw more Fresno police officers pulling up to the curb. The sergeant from the Fresno Police Department began to question me.

"Did you have a lot to drink tonight?"

"Yes," I replied.

"Were you at the bar next door, Wilkers?"

"Yes, I was with my partner."

The sergeant then advised me that there where several complaints from women that I was grabbing their butts! I was bewildered. I explained I was weaving through the crowd as I left, certainly bumping people, but certainly not grabbing any butts. The sergeant then asked for my ID, where I was employed, and if I was driving.

I surrendered my driver license, advised him that I was not driving that night and that I was a correctional officer for the Department of Corrections at Corcoran State Prison. Just as Jesse showed up, the sergeant told his officer to place me in handcuffs. I was escorted to the police cruiser and told to lean against the front bumper.

This was the first time I had ever been placed in handcuffs. *So this is what it feels like*, I thought. I was then placed in the back on the patrol cruiser and advised that I was not being arrested. I was however, brought down to the county jail for public intoxication and placed in a holding cell.

At some point, while worrying about the future of my job status and my transfer, I fell asleep only to be woken up by an officer yelling out my name and that I was being released. Jesse had called a friend of his that had come to pick me up. At that point, it was about one in the morning. Still drunk, I had to call the watch commander to inform him that I would not be reporting for duty that morning. He was already informed of the situation and instructed me to write a report of the details that occurred that night and give it to the custody captain of the Level IV SHU area. All weekend I was pacing back and forth in my apartment. My fate was in the hands of the custody captain, who was rumored to be a no non-sense, by-the-book individual.

That Monday morning I reported to my post in the SHU Kitchen at four o'clock in the morning. It was already buzzing around the SHU Units what had happened to me over the weekend. Later, Sergeant Grandy entered the SHU Kitchen with a pissed off face and a hard stare directed towards me. He pointed at me and motioned for me into his office. Once he cleared the office of all staff, he let it rip.

"What were you thinking man? The captain is very upset and has not decided what to do with you yet. You put yourself in a bind, was it worth it?"

Then the kitchen phone rang, it was the captain's secretary stating the captain wanted to see me in his office immediately. Sergeant Grandy gave me a heads up saying he and the captain go way back and for me not to bullshit him or he would have my ass!

Captain Giles had a flat top and a dip of chewing tobacco in his mouth.

"So was it worth it?"

"No, Sir."

"Officer Vodicka, I have heard nothing but good things about you. You have been doing an outstanding job running my SHU kitchen and your supervisor and I go way back. He is vouching for you by sticking his neck out on a limb; you're a lucky young man, now get the hell out of my office and good luck down in the new prison."

Calipatria State Prison sat on three hundred acres. It opened in January 1992, but the activation staff, which I was assigned to, had to be there a month early before the first buses arrived with inmates. We had to sweep the yards with metal detectors to look for metal objects that the inmates could find and make into weapons. We had to conduct security checks of the inside perimeter, making sure there was no escape route for inmates to discover, and set up the housing units with mattresses and other materials. We all had to qualify at the range with all of the lethal and non-lethal weapons along with Pr-24 training. We sat through several classroom presentations about the prison and finally, we met the new warden, Bud Prunty.

At my first opportunity I applied for the ISU Squad. This was the Investigative Services Unit I saw at my last prison; they had freedom to roam the prison and look for crime inside the walls. The selection process was long and tedious, supervised by Captain Roderick Hickman, my old commander at the academy. My file from Corcoran was evaluated, I was required to pass a series of tests and I was interviewed by the warden and the captain of the Investigative Services Unit, along with the squad sergeant. One question I remember was: *Would I ignore a guard beating up a prisoner?*

I answered in a stern voice, "No."

It must have been an answer they liked because I was chosen, one of six out of two hundred applicants. I called my parents and informed them about my new job.

After weeks of training in the Investigative Services Unit, my first assignment was as the IMARS Officer. I.M.A.R.S is known as: Inmate Monitoring and Recording System. It was an isolated room with no windows and a solid steel door that required a Folger's Adam prison key to gain entry.

At Calipatria, the inmates would have telephones inside their housing units and any outbound calls would have to be made as a collect call. There were hundreds of hours stored on large reels of tape for a twenty-four hour period. The tapes had to be replaced every day of the week. This also meant I had to come in on the weekends and replace the tapes. This machine was very useful in apprehending drugs from entering the prison by visitors and for tracking gang related business on the streets, which helped local law enforcement.

It was here, while working at Calipatria, that I met my first wife, Diane*. In 1993, after dating for over a year we were married and trying to settle into our new life together. Shortly after, we visited her family in Oregon and surprisingly we fell in love with the area. Monitoring tapes in the IMARS back at Calipatria wasn't exactly what I expected; it turned out to be a major disappointment. So when Diane introduced the idea of moving to Oregon, I was all for it. I also knew there was a state-of-the-art maximum prison recently built in the area; Pelican Bay State Prison was nestled in the tall redwoods on the California and Oregon coastline. It was in Crescent City, California, the last stop before you enter the Oregon border on the coast line.

About a year later in March of 1994, I transferred when Diane was pregnant with our son. I knew change was coming; we were moving to a new home and I was going to be a father. For these reasons alone, I expected my life was about to become hectic, but I was terribly wrong.

*denotes names change

CHAPTER SEVEN

THE STABBING

When Governor Deukmejian dedicated Pelican Bay State Prison in 1989, he proudly called it, "The prison of the future." It was a prototype for what came to be known as the "supermax" prison—an inward-facing fortress that had one thousand invincible concrete cells in the largest security housing unit ever built to entomb California's worst gangsters for their rest of their lives. Located in the northwestern part of the state near Crescent City, Del Norte County, Pelican Bay sits on 275 acres. It is in a remote forested area eleven miles from the California-Oregon state line and far from California's major metropolitan areas.

In the SHU, prisoners were generally allowed out of their cells for only one hour a day; often they were kept in solitary confinement. They received their meals through food ports located in the doors of their cells. Inmates were under constant surveillance, usually with closed-circuit television cameras. When supermax inmates were allowed to exercise, it took place in a small, enclosed area where the inmate exercised alone.

With just six years as a correctional officer, this was my third prison; I was hoping this was my last prison and that I could call it home. During my orientation, I ran into my old friend from Corcoran State Prison, Joe Reynoso. Joe was wearing sergeant's stripes; he was in charge of the Investigative Services Unit. After orientation I was assigned to a relief position on second watch, from six in the morning until two in the afternoon. I had Tuesday and Wednesday off. One day, I received a phone call in my SHU gun position by Sergeant Reynoso asking me if I wanted a job with him on the Investigative Services Unit as an evidence officer. My answer was of course, yes. I was now, one of seven squad members—six men and one woman—in the ISU. I was ecstatic to be part of the team.

On October 23, 1994, Diane went into labor at Sutter Coast Hospital. Doctor Silver delivered our little boy named Daulton*. Later that morning, Joe and his wife Les came to visit us at the hospital. True to form and as my new boss, Joe told me to take a few weeks off to spend time with my wife and son.

Upon my return, there couldn't be a worse day for collecting evidence. I had been sitting in the Evidence Room, catching up on the endless backlog of forms and reports that modern law enforcement entails. My radio scanner monitored the four different frequencies used by yard officers in the four sectors of the enormous prison. That's when I heard the urgent voice of the B Yard lieutenant on the B yard channel, "We have a stabbing on Bravo yard, and I need the squad!"

I was on my feet reaching for my evidence kit before the loudspeaker in the hallway honked and blared, "Code 3, Bravo yard, Code 3." This was the emergency code, declared by Central Control and heard over speakers throughout the prison, alerting all officers they might be needed elsewhere. Every prisoner in Pelican Bay was expected to lie down immediately if they were outside or freeze in place if indoors.

Sergeant Reynoso stepped from his office into the squad room.

"Who have I got?"

Five men came to their doorways and answered, "I'm here."

"Let's move," said Reynoso.

As we ran through the building, Reynoso was on his radio to Central Control, informing them our location so they could unlock the doors in front of us. By the time the last big gate to B Yard swung open, five minutes had elapsed since the victim's scream announced the stabbing. Outside, a cold winter rain drummed on my head, drops as big as marbles splattered over everything, washing away my crime scene. An inmate had been stabbed in the jugular—which surely produced a geyser of bright red blood—but already it was almost gone. I barely had time to pull out a swab-stick to soak up some pinkish water before it washed away.

The victim, a skinny Hispanic man, writhed and kicked on a gurney nearby.

"No me dejas morir," he pleaded. "Don't let me die, please!"

As the med techs pushed him toward the B yard clinic, they held down his arms to keep him from pulling out the shank that still protruded from his neck.

A dozen other inmates lay face down on the flooded cement basketball court, hands webbed behind their heads; one of them was the stabber. Usually when an attacker stabs someone in the neck, they will get the victim's blood somewhere on their body or clothing, but these guys were all wearing yellow vinyl raincoats provided by the state of California, the same raincoats supplied to local fire departments—coats made with silicon to make them ultra slick. Any blood spatter ran right off in the downpour; there wasn't a red speck on any of them, not even on the victim.

The guy had obviously been stabbed by one of his own. Inmates on the yard segregated themselves according to race and gang, and all the men sprawled on the court were Hispanics. Their gang allegiance would be determined as soon as squad officers got a look at their tattoos, but there were only two possibilities. The other Hispanic gangs, as well as the few whites, blacks, and Asians who ventured outside on this miserable day, were all fifty away in separate corners of the yard—like always. They too, were face down in their yellow raincoats, but the officers paid them no attention. They never would have gotten close enough to stab one of these gangsters without provoking a full-blown riot.

I was now snapping pictures with the Canon Rebel digital camera that the California Department of Corrections bought for evidence documentation. The victim by now had been identified by the med techs, as Inmate C-99777, otherwise known as John Martinez. He was unconscious and oozing blood from the homemade knife in his neck, but neither of the techs wanted to try extracting it. Instead they called for an ambulance from nearby Crescent City. ISU squad member Jimmy McMillian was assigned to stay with the victim in case he said who attacked him.

I was intrigued. John Martinez was convicted of kidnapping and rape with a deadly weapon in January, 1985, and sentenced to twenty-five years. I'd never heard of John Martinez but C inmate numbers were rare these days—like coming across a Brooklyn Dodgers baseball card. Most of the prisoners I had dealt with were F's, G's or H's. When California's prisons were reorganized and the Department of Corrections established in the mid-1940's, they started handing out five-digit inmate numbers with an A prefix. When the hundred-thousandth man entered prison they moved on to the B's. Charles Manson became Inmate B-33920 when he was sent to San Quentin in April, 1971.

The state had taken forty years to work through the first three letters of the alphabet, then just ten years to exhaust the next five. This was nearly a seven hundred percent increase in inmates per year. It was a crackdown of historic proportions and created an epic population boom in California's prisons.

The original Mexican mafia (EME) was formed in the Duel Vocational Institute of the California Prison System in Tracy, California. Between 1957 – 1960, Twenty Mexican Americans from East Los Angeles formed the core of the gang and originally named California gang the "Mexikanemi Science Temple of the Atzlan", a religious group that worshipped an ancient pre-Hispanic creed (cultural heritage). As the organization grew, it rapidly changed into a criminal organization involved in extortion, narcotics trafficking, and murder both inside and outside the prison walls.

Between 1960 -1967, the California prison system became aware of the Mexikanemi's criminal activity, broke the group up and relocated them to different prisons. Active recruitment continued by the Mexican mafia, as they are now called, and the gang basically took control of the California prisons.

For me, on this rainy day, it took the form of a dozen sullen Hispanic gang-bangers glowering back at me while I snapped their pictures. It was certain one of them had punched that shank into Martinez' neck, but I knew that none of them would ever tell who. Cooperative witnesses didn't come to Pelican Bay. I examined all of their hands and arms for a trace of blood or cuts but saw nothing suggestive. Then I called over the yard officers to help with the strip search.

The strip search is a prison ceremony that makes everyone queasy. Guards and prisoners alike consider it degrading, disgusting, and shameful—making it the perfect ritual to symbolize the vulgar intimacy of prison life. When a prisoner bends over and spreads his cheeks, he is more naked but no less embarrassed than the officer required to peer up his rectum. But the range of articles that criminals have managed to conceal in their anal cavity has astounded medical professionals for years, so good law enforcement makes the inspection necessary. That six-inch piece of sharpened metal sticking from Martinez' neck was less than an hour ago hidden up one of these inmate's rectums. Unfortunately, it was my job to search them for clues.

In the pouring rain and winter cold, a dozen inmates were ordered to strip to their boxer shorts. Then one at a time they quickly dropped drawers, bent over, and spread their cheeks; most had done it so often it became a practiced single motion. At this time however, because this was more than a routine search, an embellishment was added; they had to squat and cough simultaneously, inducing a burp than can dislodge objects inserted too deeply to see otherwise.

No incriminating evidence was discovered by this exercise; although, a lurid gallery of body art was put on display when the men stripped down. The same impulse that drives young wannabe gangsters to spray-paint the walls of their neighborhoods inspires them as adults to cover their bodies with intricate, fantastic tattoos. The tats proclaim their allegiance to the neighborhood gang. All of the men on the basketball court wore elaborate representations of the number *13* and the letter *M*—the thirteenth letter—which marked them as belonging to La Eme, the Mexican Mafia—the oldest prison gang in America and the most powerful.

A radio check confirmed that Inmate Martinez also had Eme tattoos; some faded enough to indicate long allegiance. He had been ambulanced to the small local hospital in Crescent City, where none of the doctors wanted to chance removing the shank from his neck either. Arrangements were made for a helicopter to fly him down the coast to the next larger hospital in Arcadia.

The idea of the gang standing by while one of their own was attacked didn't shock any of the squad officers. But it definitely raised their interest in John Martinez who must have seriously crossed someone important.

The green light to stab another gang member could only come from high in the ranks and would only have been decided after a consultation among the bosses. All of the known bosses however, were in isolation cells to prevent exactly that sort of communication.

The picture became somewhat clearer that evening after the yard was released, when Gang Investigative Sergeant Craig Atwater pulled the jacket for Inmate C-99777. Martinez had been in prison for ten years but only transferred to Pelican Bay in October, three months ago. Prior to that, he was at Folsom Prison, the prison for old-school convicts. Convicts of that era typically had learned how to do their time quietly, without incident, and didn't always get along with the new breed of in-your-face gangsters.

Friday morning, Sergeant Atwater spoke to his counterpart at Folsom who told him that Martinez had indeed "debriefed"—the CDC term for becoming a snitch. Likely he'd gotten on the wrong side of a gang honcho, or failed to follow an order, or simply tired of the gang life; whatever the reason, he had told prison officials everything he knew about Eme activities at Folsom. In return he'd been promised a good word when he came up for parole and moved to Pelican Bay for his protection. This was terminal naiveté all around, since the gang could play the system as well as the authorities with equal or better intelligence but far more ruthless conviction. It had taken three months for the gang to discover Martinez' betrayals, decide his fate, track him down, and find somebody to stab him.

Their determination to finish the job was made clear that afternoon, when a Hispanic male called the warden's office, claiming to be a member of Martinez' family and wanting to know what hospital he'd been moved to. Martinez' family however, had not yet been notified that anything had happened to him. The gang knew more than they did.

The ISU Squad was on the road that night and by dawn Saturday they were at Mad River Community Hospital in Arcadia to provide a "roving patrol" in case an Eme hit-team showed up from L.A. The doctors there had finally managed to extract the shank, but Martinez slipped into a coma. When I took my turn watching over him the man looked awful; his neck was dark purple and so swollen that the surgery staples were pulling loose. He died Sunday morning.

Early the next week I visited the cells occupied by the dozen inmates from the basketball court. I had the murder weapon with me, a six-inch strip of steel band, less than an inch wide; it was probably thrown over the wall from the prison metal shop. It was sharpened to a blunt but effective point and had a scrap of white cotton t-shirt wrapped around it for a handle. I found what I was looking for in Housing Unit 3 of cellblock B.

On the gray cement wall behind the bolted-down toilet in cell B3-110, were heavy scratch marks where someone had laboriously filed a piece of metal recently. The shank from Martinez' neck matched the scratches exactly. I snapped pictures and scraped metal flakes into a small plastic sample container for lab analysis, which I doubted would be necessary. One of the cell's two occupants was merely an accomplice who could be downgraded to a witness with some serious coaxing; eventually he was.

The cell's other occupant was Inmate H-47645, a twenty-two-year-old gang-banger named Jaime Ponce who was down for transport and possession of a controlled substance with intent to sell; a routine drug bust that bought him five years. Most short-timers his age would have been assigned to a less formidable prison than Pelican Bay, but Ponce made the grade because he was a known active gang member. His standing in the Eme however wasn't quite as glorious as the prosecutors thought.

When he pleaded guilty to first degree murder, Ponce admitted that he'd been "in the hat"—in trouble with the gang—and killed Martinez to clear himself. He wouldn't say what the trouble was, but it gave the Eme more leverage over him than the State of California could wield. At the time of the killing he had only two more years to serve before being released; instead he would spend the rest of his days at Pelican Bay. It was a measure of the fear and control the gang enjoys inside the prison, where gang values rule and everyone's safety depends on abiding by them. Ponce and Martinez both knew those rules when they made their choices, and the brutal law of prison decided their fate— one was blood in for life, the other was blood out.

The EME uses killings as a means of discipline or gaining respect. EME killings are extremely gruesome and calculated to establish fear and intimidation.

The lesson wasn't lost for me; I collected evidence every day on the fatal consequence of snitching in prison. I never imagined that someday I'd be "in the hat" myself, forced to make those fearsome choices and tempt that same fate.

Chapter Eight

The Gassing

It was just past our two year anniversary when my marriage began to crumble. Diane complained about our location, we were living in a small town right on the coast of Oregon called Brookings. It was a small lumber town with a population of about 5,400. She said it was too cold and rainy, and that she was starting to get cabin fever.

"I have no friends up here and you are always at work; your pager goes off in the middle of the night and you have to respond back to the prison. I never see you anymore D. J."

She wanted to leave the area and be closer to her other two children from her previous marriage, who were living in Gilroy, California with there biological father. She told me one morning that she was going to take Daulton and go stay with her mother in Williams, Oregon. I knew I had to do something quick; I didn't want to lose her and my little boy.

As a correctional officer, there are many stressors in the work environment. We live by a "macho code" that requires us to be rugged individuals. The macho code combined with the unpredictability of working with inmates, role ambiguity, and demographic changes in the work force create high stress levels. A correctional officer has twice the national divorce rate average, high rates of suicide, alcoholism, and heart attacks. According to a recent study, the average life span for someone with this occupation is fifty years compared to a national average of seventy-five years. It is said correctional officers may respond to stress by engaging in corruption or inmate brutality.

One day, I was sitting in the lunch room in the administration building getting ready to eat lunch, when I had to respond to an urgent call over the walkie-talkies. I jumped in my squad vehicle and headed towards the SHU. Once inside, I was walking down the long corridor where Delta 3 Housing

Unit was located when I began to smell a foul odor. I noticed a trail of a brown substance on the corridor floor coming from the direction of Delta 3. I stopped immediately and I knew what I was responding to collect. I reached into my cargo pocket of my green jumpsuit for my small jar of Vicks. I dipped my finger into the jar and rubbed it under my nose above my upper lip, this way I would only smell the Vicks and not what I was expecting to find when I entered the unit.

I continued to follow the brown liquid trail to B pod, where the trail lead right to cell 105. It was a "gassing" of the staff. A gassing was when an inmate would urinate and defecate into a cup and let it sit for days, then as an officer walked by their cell doors, the inmate would throw the cup of waste at the officer. The Vicks was no use; I ran towards the officer's bathroom and vomited into the toilet. I washed my face with cold water, regained my composure, and placed more Vicks onto my upper lip and even in my nostrils. I collected two pint size paper cups full of feces. I secured the lids and placed each one separately into a brown evidence bag. Then, I marked the areas that needed to be marked for evidential purposes later, for trial. Upon exiting the cell, I noticed that there were more splashes of feces on the walls leading up towards the gunner's control booth. I realized this happened *outside of the cell*, but how?

I immediately headed to the gunner's control room; there, I observed more feces spread all over the upper walls and the control panel. I swabbed and marked accordingly, placing the additional evidence into individual containers for processing.

Finally, in the Medical Clinic, I observed Correctional Officer Craig Donnahoe standing in his green colored jumpsuit covered with feces from head to toe. Donnahoe was beyond livid but stood still long enough for me to photograph him for evidence. I collected his jumpsuit and his protective vest and placed them into separate brown bags for processing later in the Squad Room. I went back to the holding cells where the inmates were being held who committed the assault on Donnahoe. They were two black inmates, inmate Manago and inmate Mathews. I photographed both of them while they where in the holding cage for identification purposes later in trial. The trial lasted a full week. The evidence was clear in this case and the jury found Manago guilty. Mathews took a plea bargain when he found out that Manago was found guilty. He knew his fate would have been decided before he reached the court room.

I got wind that another prison was opening in Monterey, California, called Salinas Valley State Prison; a Level IV Prison scheduled to open the first of the year in 1996.

Headquartered out of Sacramento, California, Salinas Valley State Prison was scouting for seasoned veteran officers like me—with level IV experience—to apply for the Activation Team. This would give me a third notch on my belt for activating a new prison and more importantly, a way to try to salvage my marriage.

Diane was thrilled to hear the news; the new prison was close to her family in Gilroy. I submitted my transfer to Salinas Valley State Prison while Diane stayed with her mother and step father in Williams, Oregon.

I finally received my notice in the mail from headquarters to report to Salinas Valley State Prison on Monday, March 1, 1996 in Class A Uniform. It was a very emotional day when I said good-bye to all of my coworkers, the warden, and especially my good friend Joe Reynoso and his wife Les.

"ENTRANCE GATE TO SALINAS VALLEY STATE PRISON"

Chapter Nine

The Riot

Salinas Valley State Prison was the first prison to open after California passed its famous "Three Strikes" law. As a result of the new law, the place was instantly filled to double capacity with career criminals sentenced to life with no possibility of parole; they were all angry hopeless men. The place turned into chaos within weeks; assault records were broken in months and *seven* wardens arrived and departed in two years.

The whole flawed strategy of California's—and America's—thirty year war on crime had come to a head at Salinas Valley. Passing even harsher laws had swept millions of law-breakers off the streets and into over-crowded, under-funded prisons where gangs controlled the yards and imposed gang rules. All pretenses of rehabilitation were abandoned in the 1990's, not just in California but nationwide, turning prisons into crime schools that sent their embittered alumni back to helpless neighborhoods.

Salinas Valley State Prison opened in May, 1996 at a cost of 236 million dollars, with an annual budget of 177 million dollars. The prison covered more than three hundred acres. It was the sixth maximum security prison built in California since Corcoran set the mold just eight years earlier. I helped activate three of these maximum prisons. I was now a skilled veteran in a vital industry.

When I arrived at the Salinas Valley, it was the same routine as when I started my first day at Corcoran State Prison almost eight years ago in 1988. I entered the orientation room and pointed out the fish cops—their uniforms highly pressed and there boots shinned. As for me, I walked in wearing my Class "A" Uniform, with yellow hash marks indicating my years of service with the CDC. There were only a handful of seasoned veterans that transferred to Salinas Valley State Prison.

During orientation, I met Captain Robert Padilla, who was with the Parole Division and took a liking to me very quickly. After hearing of my professional background, he asked me to join his ISU Squad. This would be my third stint in an Investigative Services Unit.

I dug the yard and swept the cells with other veteran officers, preparing the prison for the new convicts. At the same time, Captain Padilla had asked me to start setting up the Investigative Services Unit and order all the equipment it needed to function.

In June of 1996, the first inmates arrived at Salinas Valley State Prison. The big green and black buses were lined up outside the perimeter fence filled with inmates ready to be processed into the prison. Not to my surprise, a problem had already arisen on the first day.

There were two inmates in the holding cages that were refusing to come off the bus because they did not request to be transferred to Salinas; they added that they would put up a fight if they had to. The other inmates trickled off the bus one at a time, wearing their orange jumpsuits with the leg shackles around their ankles and waist chains with both hands cuffed to their sides.

Investigative Sergeant Rocha turned to me and said, "Come with me Vodicka."

We approached the first cage, where a skinny black inmate was refusing to exit the bus. I suppose after taking note of my size, he immediately surrendered, allowing me to remove him from the bus. The second was an obese, sweaty, white inmate. He stunk terribly as if he had not bathed in a month. I hated the idea of having to get physical with him, but before I even got to him, he surrendered as well. I remember the buses were dropping off inmates daily until the prison was at its full capacity, which only took about three months.

The total population grew to about four thousand inmates to about six hundred officers. There were four yards, lettered A, B, C, and D. Each yard was able to house one thousand inmates. A majority of the inmates were in prison for life and unfortunately, we did not get the "programmable" inmates; we received the "shit" inmates, who were the problem children at other institutions; exiled by the warden. Basically, we were the dumping grounds for the worst of the worst—the most violent and unbearable inmates.

In the first year alone, Salinas Valley State Prison had the most incident reports in the state of California. All incidents were considered felonies and reported to the local District Attorney for possible prosecution; the inmate can be found guilty or not guilty and receive more time onto there current sentence.

Salinas Valley State Prison had so many violent episodes the media took notice, airing several segments about the prison. The B yard soon became so brutal that the guards started calling it, "Little Beirut." Inmates guilty of child molestation, were a high target for other inmates. Many were beaten beyond recognition, stabbed, had their heads bashed in, bones broken—left to bleed to death on B yard. One child molester was so terrified of the other inmates, he dove headfirst from his upper bunk into his cell's steel toilet, breaking his neck and leaving brain fragments inside the cell.

As the lead ISU officer, to say my hands were full was an understatement. The daily violence I had to endure and the brutality I was in charge of investigating left me miserable. The constant stress was a poison to my spirit and my marriage. In a last-ditch effort to save my sanity and my marriage, I asked to be released from ISU. I demoted myself and took a job as an ordinary line guard with regular hours and limited responsibilities.

The damage however, was already past repair. On Halloween night, after an exhausting day at work, I was happy to spend time with my son, Daulton, who was now three and dressed like a pumpkin. Later that night, after tucking him in to bed, Diane dropped the bomb on me.

"D. J. I don't love you anymore and I am asking for a peaceful divorce. You can keep the house, I'll be moving out with Daulton. You can have visiting rights anytime."

●　　　●　　　●

On Thanksgiving Day, 1998, as a result of being denied of his request to enter the building to utilize the telephone, an inmate by the name of Hernandez, began to kick the building's back door. Officers Chargualaf and Cerda approached Hernandez in an attempt to reprimand him, at which point he became highly agitated, boisterous, and hostile towards them. He was ordered to submit to a clothed body search, but Hernandez only became increasingly rowdy to deliberately gain the attention of the surrounding inmates. As a result of his defiance, Hernandez was placed in handcuffs and prepared to be escorted to the sergeant's office.

Suddenly, all of the Hispanic inmates on the yard stopped what they were doing. Together, they emptied from the handball court, left the basketball court and pull bar area, all proceeding quickly towards Building 7, where Hernandez was being held.

Officers Peterson, Ruiz, Reese and Officer Castroena took notice and tried to intercept the approaching Hispanic inmates. Their efforts went ignored. Officer Reese immediately contacted the gun tower officer and instructed him to put the yard down. The firm command came loudly through the yard's speakers. Again, orders were ignored by the Hispanic inmates.

All the other inmates obeyed and were lying face down; the Hispanic gang was now blatantly refusing all orders. Sergeant Brandon then attempted to

defuse and de-escalate the situation by instructing one Hispanic "spokesman"—
the shot-caller—to step forward and the remaining inmates to step back and
assume the prone position. Inmate Flores approached Sergeant Brandon.
The other Hispanic inmates refused to take the prone position and remained
standing. Then, pausing for just a moment as if to act in unison, the Hispanic
inmates moved in on the correctional staff.

Correctional Lieutenant G. Lewis ordered the tower to fire one warning
shot into the grass beside the inmates. A final order was given, for all inmates
to assume the prone position. Hispanic inmates towards the back of the group
began to prone out, while approximately thirteen others remained standing.

Then, through the tense silence, two inmates yelled, "Let's get them, it's
on!"

Like a stampede, the inmates rushed towards the staff and began to unleash
their fury. At some point during the attack, Officer Chargualaf lost possession
of his PR-24 side handle baton. Inmate Holloway gained control of the baton
and struck Officer Narvaez to the right side of the head, knocking him to the
ground.

Inmate Mania stood up and began yelling for all inmates to get up and attack
staff. As officers attempted to handcuff inmates, they were being attacked from
behind. A large group of inmates got up from the prone position and began to
run toward the staff when Officer Morris fired his federal 37mm launcher from
his control booth position. The wooden baton rounds blasted into the inmates
as they attacked. They immediately dropped to the ground.

Additional responding staff began to arrive from other yards of the prison
and physically began forcing all inmates into the prone position and restraining
them on the ground. Temporary Flex-Cuffs were retrieved from the program
office and applied to the hands and feet of each inmate to prevent further
attacks. There must have been fifty officers, myself included, who responded.
For the first time, I saw was force of *green*.

The attack injured eighteen officers; fourteen were transported to Salinas
Valley Memorial Hospital. Once the situation was under control, Lieutenant
Lewis asked me if I would retrieve the crime camera kit from Complex Control
and initiate the collection of evidence and photographs.

I heard sirens coming into the prison; there were several outside ambulances
agencies taking staff to the hospital for further medical evaluation and I knew
eventually I would have to respond to the hospital and photograph injuries
there as well.

There were several Hispanic inmates restrained on the yard. I photographed
them at point of discovery. Then, they were rolled over on their backs, where
several of them revealed they were lying on top of inmate-manufactured

stabbing weapons meant to be used on the staff. Those were also photographed at point of discovery and then placed into an evidence bag.

As the inmates were brought in from the yard, I noticed many of them had abrasions to their face, neck, and body. I began taking photographs of them to document their injuries as well. By the looks I was getting from my fellow guards, they seemed to be confused as to why I was doing this—documenting *inmate* injuries. I was just doing my job, what I had been asked to do by my lieutenant.

"What the fuck are you doing Vodicka?" Officer Faulkner asked. Officer Ivanich peered at me, waiting for my answer.

I was confused, but responded, "Just doing my job."

On November 26, 1998, the riot that broke out at Salinas State Valley Prison made headlines nationwide. To this day, it is remembered by the staff still working at the prison, by wearing turkey pins on their uniforms.

This is also the day that the trust between me and the other officers would be broken. Specifically, I was the one not to be trusted by any staff. This was the day of the forming of the "Green Wall." The group went underground for almost three years with the group starting small. It then grew very rapidly and resurfaced in the year 2001 when we received our new warden.

"PERMITER GUARD TOWER"
SALINAS VALLEY STATE PRISON

CHAPTER TEN

THE INVESTIGATION BEGINS

In March of 2001, I was the video camera operator for three cell extractions that took place on Facility D yard. On video and before the cell extraction, each officer had to identify who themselves, give their badge number and state their specific job during the extraction. My taping caught an officer named Michael Ruiz flashing a gang sign that looked like a "W;" it was later determined as a symbol for the "Green Wall." As a result, Officer Ruiz was removed from the Special Emergency Response Team (SERT) and put under investigation by Internal Affairs Sergeant Azell Middlebrooks. Rumors began to swirl that I "told on him" to the administration concerning his hand gestures. Rather than confronting me about the issue, Officer Ruiz did nothing but hold a grudge towards me. I knew the investigation on Officer Ruiz, would be the start of me being a "marked man" at the prison. The change in my coworker's attitudes toward me was extremely obvious. Cold shoulders, stale greetings, avoidance of eye contact, rushed small talk—if any—and an overall feeling of isolation.

One day, during my annual range training, as I entered the classroom to sign in, Officer Ruiz quickly proceeded to the back room where the other range instructors were, told them of my presence and instructed them to talk about something else. Clearly, he was holding me responsible for his removal from SERT. In another incident with Ruiz, his resentment towards me grew bolder. As I approached the handle baton training area, Officer Ruiz made a slashing motion across his neck to another officer as I passed by. When I asked him why he did it, he ignored me and walked away. I knew this problem was only going to get worse. I was not going to stand for continued harassment, nor wait for bolder acts of aggression to begin. I documented everything that happened at the range and brought a copy of my report to the Employee Relations Office. I gave it to Lieutenant Vertis Elmore, who worked directly for the warden.

I was hoping it would all just blow over. Then, one particular evening, I hoped on one of the golf carts that transported officers to the exit at the prison's main entrance. A few other officers were headed in my direction so I asked the driver to stop and signaled for them to hop on.

"Go ahead, we'll wait for you to come back and pick us up."

And there it was; the confirmation that I was officially an outcast. I was considered a rat—enemy.

The "Green Wall" was growing tremendously at the prison and their rebellious behavior was out of control. They placed contraband in inmates' cells, used unnecessary force at will, and became middle men for drug and weapon transfers within the prison. Any staff members who attempted to interfere with their actions were verbally threatened and/or had their vehicle damaged. Flattened tires and more commonly "GW" or "7/23" was keyed into their car— 7/23 stood for the seventh letter of the alphabet, G, and the 23rd letter of the alphabet, W—initials of the "Green Wall." Although correctional officers belonging to the "Green Wall" followed the Code of Silence, an unspoken agreement in which they would not disclose or report the inappropriate and illegal activity of other correctional officers, how they were conducting their business against inmates and staff was no secret.

Soon after, the Office of the Inspector General (OIG) initiated an Administrative Investigation into allegations of misconduct against four California Department of Corrections correctional officers assigned to the ISU at the prison. The allegations were made by an inmate named Richardo Tellez, who was the "shot caller" for Facility C yard. These four officers were to be investigated for using unnecessary and/or excessive force against Tellez during a cell search on April 3, 2001. Tellez also alleged that these officers planted an inmate-manufactured weapon in his cell, falsified reports, and stole property belonging to him during the search.

Lieutenant Robert Kim of the Internal Affairs Unit at the prison phoned the Office of the Inspector General and asked if they wanted to conduct their own independent investigation into the matter. The OIG accepted the offer.

In a video-taped interview conducted by Lieutenant Mark Treadwell, inmate Richardo Tellez alleged that ISU Officers Walter Faulkner, Michael Lashkoff, Anthony Ivanich, and Fernando Chavez used unnecessary and/or excessive force on him during a cell search on April 3, 2001. According to his *Inmate CDC 602 Grievance Report*, the four named officers rushed into his cell throwing him to the ground and stuck their knee in his back and neck area. They then twisted his legs until he screamed in horrific pain. Tellez also claimed that he was in mechanical restraints—handcuffs—and that he was not resisting when all of this was took place.

As a result of the independent investigation, the charges were sustained by the OIG; the officers were found guilty and the report was forwarded to the California Department of Corrections for disciplinary action.

At this point in time, I was working in the Vehicle Sally Port, checking incoming and outgoing vehicles that entered the prison. I received a phone call one day from Officer Garcia telling me that Officer Gibbons, Vice President of the prison's union, was walking around with a special agent from the Office of Internal Affairs from Sacramento. The investigator was going around to each officer's station and asking them if they ever heard of the "Green Wall." He informed me that if I said yes, they would record my name and question me further. He then, instructed me to say no, that I had never heard of the "Green Wall."

The special agent never stopped by the Vehicle Sally Port.

One morning, at my usual stop by the Watch Office on the way to the Sally Port, Lieutenant G. Lewis, who was now assigned to the ISU as the Internal Affairs Lieutenant, said he needed to speak with me.

We stepped into his office and he asked me to close the door as he shut the blinds on his windows—which I knew would raise the eyebrows of anyone who saw me enter. Lieutenant Lewis and I were not only coworkers, we were friends. We had known each other for years; we both worked at Pelican Bay State Prison together. We also transferred to Salinas Valley State Prison together with our families and we both lived at Lake Naciemento, often car pooling with each other to the prison. Lieutenant Lewis was aware of my strong background with the ISU.

He sat down in his chair, pulled a document out from his top drawer and pushed it towards me, asking me to read it. I knew I was not authorized to read the document and told him that, at which point he stated firmly that he *wanted* me to read it. The document was a *California Department of Corrections Form 989*, an Internal Affairs Investigation request. Lieutenant Lewis wanted a Category II Investigation, meaning that *Sacramento* would conduct an investigation from the Office of Internal Affairs and *not* Salinas Valley State Prison itself. An outside agency performing the investigation avoided a feared internal cover up. I grabbed the document, slumped back into my chair and began to read. The narrative read as follows:

> On June 27, 2001, Salinas Valley State Prison ISU Lieutenant Lewis summarized his review of documents and information surrounding the group of SVSP staff who associate themselves with the number "7/23", which stands for the "Green Wall." The following are recent incidents that have occurred at SVSP showing the group is active and growing in numbers.

In January 2001, several staff had signed their FSLA's with green ink, a symbol of association or support of the group. Sometime after Lieutenant Lewis' assignment to the ISU, he observed a security squad officer with a box of green ink pens on his desk with a sign that read, "Take one if you dare."

On May 29, 2001, it was discovered that security squad officers had brought a green-colored knife into the institution as a gift for the departing ISU sergeant. Engraved on the knife was the number "7/23." After removal of the involved staff from ISU, there have been reports of vandalized vehicles.

When the "7/23" group was first identified in 1999, there was an unconfirmed concern that the "Green Wall" stood for the Code of Silence and that members practiced intimidation of other staff. The only sign of the group's activity were some management memos and facility property that had "7/23" written on them, some in green ink.

This investigation is requested to determine if this group has involved itself in acts of misconduct and if they are a threat to the safety and security of the institution.

Lewis informed me that our prison's warden, Warden Anthony Lamarque, refused to sign off on the Internal Affairs investigation, so Chief Deputy Warden Bobby Hernandez, second in command, signed for Lamarque.

I was curious; Lamarque must have been hiding something concerning the "Green Wall," but I could not put my finger on it. Why wouldn't he sign off on something as serious as this? The Category II Investigation request was approved by the Assistant Director of the Office of Internal Affairs.

Lewis then asked me to document what I had seen and the phone call I received from Officer Garcia, telling me to answer no if I was ever questioned about knowing about the "Green Wall." Staff feared Lieutenant Lewis, and no one wanted to give him any information. Although he shouldn't have been sharing this information with me, he knew that with my strong background in the ISU and years of experience in the California Department of Corrections, I was a credible source. My documentation of happenings would be crucial evidence in his report. I didn't like this, I hated the situation I had been placed in, but I couldn't ignore my ethical beliefs. Officers were abusing their power and going against the oath they had taken. I honored my badge and everything it stood for. I knew what I had to do.

CHAPTER ELEVEN

EXPOSED

On Monday, September 3, 2001, I stopped by the home of Lieutenant Lewis, where I found him very angry. He told me that when Warden Lamarque found out that he had Hernandez sign off for him on the Category II Investigation, Lamarque relieved Lewis of control from the Investigative Services Unit, making himself in command. Lewis then showed me a memorandum he wrote to Captain Miles Moore and Warden Lamarque *before* he requested the Category II Investigation:

> *From: Lieutenant Lewis*
> *To: Internal Affairs Captain Miles Moore*
> *Cc: Warden Lamarque*
>
> CONFIDENTIAL
>
> *Introduction of Weapons into the Institution,*
>
> *On May 29, 2001, I received information from Correctional Sergeant C. Donnahoe, Squad Sergeant that a knife had been brought into the institution on May 25, 2001 by Investigative Services Unit Officers A. Ivanich, W. Faulkner and M. Lashkoff. The information indicated the knife was green in color and inscribed with the numbers 7/23 (Symbolic of the group "Green Wall"). This knife was reported presented to Correctional Sergeant J. Celeya in the Investigative Services Squad Sergeants Office.*

Based upon this information, I instructed Correctional Sergeant C. Donnahoe to contact the trophy shop (Salinas Valley Trophies, Salinas CA) where the plaque was inscribed for Sergeant Celeya to ascertain if a knife was engraved. Sergeant Donnahoe made contact via telephone and confirmed a knife and plaque had been inscribed at the business.

Sergeant Donnahoe and A. Middlebrooks were dispatched to the business and obtained the original work order for the knife which indicated a description of the knife and confirmed the requested engraving of 7/23. The purchase order had the signature of Investigative Services Unit Officer W. Faulkner. The owner of the business positively identified Officer Faulkner via photograph as the individual that ordered and picked up the knife.

On May 29, 2001, I met with Warden A. Lamarque and fully apprised him of this developing information. During this meeting I re-emphasized my concerns relative to my previous discussions and requests to reassign ISU Officers, A. Ivanich, W. Faulkner and M. Lashkoff, based upon their affiliation with the group "7/23, green wall." I informed Warden Lamarque during this discussion I would be contacting Special Agent T. Knight, OIA, relevant to this occurrence based upon the open, ongoing investigation relevant to the activities of the group of Officers affiliated with the "green wall / 7/23" at Salinas Valley State Prison.

On May 29, 2001, I personally reviewed the purchase order retrieved from Salinas Valley Trophies. After this review, Myself and Sergeant Donnahoe and Middlebrooks met with Chief Deputy Warden R. Hernandez and briefed him on the occurrence. Additionally, a photocopy of the purchase order was provided to him for review and discussion with Warden Lamarque. Based upon Officer Faulkner being the assigned ISU evidence Officer, I instructed Sergeant Donnahoe to maintain possession of the purchase order. Warden Lamarque met with Sergeant Donnahoe during the afternoon and instructed him to reassign all three officers from the Investigative unit based upon this development and the evidence presented.

On Monday, June 04, 2001, I contacted Captain M. Moore, via telephone at his residence and apprised him of this knife incident. Per Captain Moore's direction, I contacted Special Agent T. knight and apprised him of the discovery of *the Introduction of the knife and purchase order. Agent knight consulted with his supervisor, Senior Special Agent J. Negrette and instructed me to mail all supporting evidence to his office.*

Lieutenant Lewis explained to me that he attempted to follow the chain of command when he wrote the memorandum to Captain Moore and Warden Lamarque, but they did nothing. As a result of their lack of action, only then did Lewis reach out to higher authorities—the Office of Internal Affairs. Not only did Lamarque relieve Lewis of control, he called Sergeant Donnahoe during that same afternoon and instructed him to reassign all three of the officers from ISU based upon the development and the evidence presented.

Finally, I thought, *it was about fucking time Lamarque did something about this.* But I wondered if Lamarque was just doing this to shut everyone up. Why only now did he take action? Was it to show Internal Affairs that he was "handling the situation" in the event they followed up with the report?

Lieutenant Lewis had asked me for my advice, not only because we were good friends, but because we trusted each other. I told him to follow his instincts and hold onto his ethical standards. If the warden wasn't going to listen to him, he could always go to the Regional Administrator with his evidence.

Eventually, Lieutenant Lewis went to the Regional Administrator. Soon after, Warden Lamarque received a phone call from Regional Administrator Richard Early, telling him that Lieutenant Lewis was transferred to Avenal State Prison and he would not be returning back to Salinas Valley State Prison. With Lieutenant Greg Lewis gone, I was the only one left to fight the battle against the "Green Wall."

On Friday, September 7, 2001, I was ordered by Warden Lamarque to prepare a report about my knowledge of any inappropriate and illegal activity by correctional officers that threatened the health or safety of inmates, employees, or the public. He specifically wanted me to include in my report what had taken place at Lieutenant Lewis' home and the report Lieutenant Lewis had me write. I wrote the report as instructed and stamped it *Confidential* on both top and bottom pages and kept a copy for myself.

I was under the impression that this report for Warden Lamarque was to assist with the investigation. Little did I know, Warden Lamarque only wanted me to write this report to reveal that Lieutenant Lewis had exposed confidential information to me. Although Lewis had good intentions, I was not authorized to know details about certain events taking place within the prison, and Lamarque fooled me into exposing Lewis.

In further attempts to make it look like they were "handling" the "Green Wall" situation, Captain Moore held a meeting with Sergeant Donnahoe and Lieutenant Kim, calling on ISU Officer Steve Archibald. In small-talk and friendly chatter, Archibald had previously shared information with me about what was going in the ISU. The sharing of information between departments was prohibited. While I was previously a part of the ISU Squad, since resigning I was now technically a Line Staff member. Since I had mentioned Archibald and details he had shared with me as evidence in my report written for Warden Lamarque, Captain Moore released him from the ISU. Even worse, during the meeting, Captain Moore intentionally left my report out on his desk, in plain sight for Archibald to see. Sergeant Donnahoe and Lieutenant Kim were shocked by the Captain's behavior, his blatant disregard for confidentiality—deliberately jeopardizing my safety.

Livid, Archibald confronted me immediately. He told me about the meeting and how he was released from the ISU, all because of me, because I ratted him out. He screamed at me—he was enraged, wild. I was confused and attempted to explain when he started quoting my exact words, words that I had written in my "confidential" report for the warden.

Now I was furious. Warden Lamarque and Captain Moore threw me right under the bus. I contacted Internal Affairs Sergeant Azell Middlebrooks at once. The minute he heard my hysterics over the phone, he met me at the Sally Port.

Middlebrooks immediately contacted his acquaintance from the Office of Inspector General, Senior Inspector General Richard Ramsdell. He set up a meeting between the two of us at a designated location away from the prison to discuss the "Green Wall" and their activities. We met that night, at a restaurant parking lot in King City, thirty miles south of the prison. I waited until a black SUV pulled alongside my vehicle. Richard Ramsdell showed me his identification and asked me if I could sit in the passenger side of his vehicle to begin the interview.

Inspector General David Grant was sitting in the back seat. Ramsdell started off by saying how he appreciated my cooperation with him and the Inspector General's Office and that this meeting would be regarded extremely confidential. He informed me of the investigation that they were conducting on the "Green Wall" at Salinas Valley State Prison and on a group of correctional officers, as well as management, that was condoning illegal activities against inmates and staff. I asked him if I was the only one that came forward about the Green Wall. Ramsdell revealed I wasn't; a certain lieutenant was also cooperating with them.

The recorded interview lasted about two hours. At the conclusion of the interview, they asked me to write down everything that I stated during the interview and to get it to them right away. Ramsdell also told me to contact him immediately if anyone threatened me, and they would move me to a safer place for my own protection.

Four months later, on Monday, January 14, 2002, six unmarked government vehicles pulled onto the prison grounds. They were from the Office of Inspector General out of Sacramento, California—working directly for the governor's office, completely independent from the California Department of Corrections.

Investigating Case #01-177 at Salinas Valley State Prison, were the following investigators and their title:

Barbara Moore, Deputy Inspector General in Charge
David Grant, Deputy Inspector General Senior
Richard Ramsdell, Deputy Inspector General Senior
David Faingold, Deputy Inspector General
Lisa Heintz, Deputy Inspector General
Ken Baird, Deputy Inspector
Tina Gonzales, Deputy Inspector
Thomas Garcia, Associate Deputy Inspector General
Gwen Warrener, Associate Deputy Inspector General

Their arrival was startling; no one, not even the warden was forewarned. As the investigators entered, they all had designated assignments. They rushed the Investigative Services Unit and instructed all officers to stop what they were doing and to leave the unit immediately; the captain of the unit included.

Later that afternoon, to my horror, I received several threatening phone calls from anonymous callers: "Vodicka, you rat, you brought the Inspector General's Office to our prison; you better watch every step you take."

I immediately called Middlebrooks to inform him I was receiving threatening calls at my post. I demanded to know what the hell was going on at the prison. Middlebrooks told me that the Inspector General's Office raided the Investigative Services Unit, looking for evidence against the "Green Wall" and certain officers affiliated with the gang. That however, wasn't the information I was looking for. *How in the hell did these anonymous officers that called me, associate me with the raid? I thought the meeting I had with Ramsdell and the Inspector General's Office was confidential.*

In the next few weeks I received three separate letters telling me to watch my back inside of the prison because staff had me as a marked man. The first letter I received was from my prior investigative partner, Officer Andy Cariaga. He informed me, that while he was on Facility "A" yard, he witnessed Officer Archibald in a serious conversation with Officer Barbuto, telling Barbuto that he was removed from ISU because of me. He continued to tell him how he even read the actual report I had written to the warden.

The second document was from Officer E. Tiller, who at the time worked in the Central Infirmary Center. According to Officer Tiller, she informed

Officer Atkins, who was her relief for the next shift, when I was due to report. She said Officer Atkins expressed ill feelings toward working with me. Further, that Officer Atkins went on to say how I "told on" Lieutenant Lewis by writing up a report on him after he revealed confidential information to me and that I was "always telling on someone." Officer Tiller informed me that Officer Atkins' statements seemed as if Atkins was going to try to cause some sort of trouble with me and she didn't want me to enter into a hostile work environment. After receiving her letter, I requested to be reassigned to the front entrance and have another officer work my position. I wanted to avoid Officer Atkins and any trouble he would try and cause me.

The last written document I received was from Sergeant Gomez:

> *This is a documented record of the discussions we had in regards to staff making off-the-cuff comments that I heard in passing claiming you are a "snitch." I have some concerns as to how this is affecting you at work and as a supervisor I must document this for your protection. Many times staff can say comments without knowing the full facts and not knowing the damage they can inflict by spreading rumors. This is why I need to inform you as to what is being said about you out of respect for you as an officer, and as a friend as well. Should you need any assistance or help please do not hesitate to contact me at any time.*

I continued to receive threatening phone calls. The word was out, everyone at the prison was aware of the situation. No one knew the details or the true story, but everyone saw me as a traitor. This was when my paranoia set in. This was when I started to constantly look over my shoulder. This was when I began checking underneath my car every morning.

Shortly after the raid, Richard Ramsdell and his team arrived back to the prison to serve subpoenas to the officers and staff that were involved with the "Green Wall;" the subpoenas went all the way up the chain of command—to the warden's office. They were to be interviewed by the Office of the Inspector General on suspected criminal behavior against inmates.

All hell had broken loose; I had to get out of the prison immediately. I was already receiving threats, my safety was compromised, and I feared what would happen next. When I advised Middlebrooks about the worsening situation and his response was for me to "chill out", I was frantic. I demanded he tell Ramsdell about what was going on. When he ignored my repeated requests, I decided to contact Ramsdell on my own.

One day, I made my way to the Administration Building to locate Ramsdell myself. In the staff cafeteria, I saw Ramsdell and his partner Inspector General David Grant. I pulled up a chair, told him about the threatening phone calls I had received and letters from fellow officers warning me, and how I now feared for my life at the prison. I was astonished when Ramsdell seemed like he didn't care what I had to say; I actually felt that he was brushing me off. I reminded him of his promise to remove me from the prison if I felt my life was in danger. Finally, Ramsdell said he would look into it right away. Days passed with no word from Ramsdell on my transfer. I felt lied to. I felt used. I contacted Middlebrooks again and told him that if he did not help me transfer from the prison, I would go over his head for help and then go to the media about what was going on at the prison.

I needed help. I contacted my old friend Joe Reynoso, who was working as a Special Agent for a unit called the Special Services Unit—the SSU was a hand-picked unit responsible for investigated all aspects of the California Department of Corrections. When I got him on the phone, I informed him of the events that took place and the situation I was in. Reynoso immediately called his boss.

Whatever Reynoso did, got the ball rolling. I received a phone call from Middlebrooks that same day asking me where I wanted to be transferred. I told Middlebrooks that I wanted to go to Pleasant Valley State Prison. I was told that Warden Lamarque was hesitant to sign off on my transfer, however once told about the bigger problems he would face if I stayed, he quickly agreed.

Chapter Twelve

The Set Up

I arrived at Pleasant Valley State Prison welcomed by Chief Deputy Warden Paul Ward, a short, gray-haired man with a smile from ear to ear. He acknowledged my years of experience in the Department of Corrections and even went so far as to say that it was a privilege to have me working at his prison. He asked if I wanted to return back to the ISU; I appreciatively decline his offer. I was placed on Facility D yard, which he indicated was the most violent yard housing all the Northern Structure Hispanic inmates in the prison.

My days at the new prison started off quite sour. While in the Watch Office, Custody Captain Ryan Williams approached me and introduced himself. He then, in front of other staff, stated that I was "the one on the victim witness program they sent here from another prison." I was offended and quickly stood up to let him have it and defend myself but realized it wasn't worth it. Not only did the staff at Pleasant Valley know about my situation, but at that moment I knew I was going to have problems here as well. Later, I found out this same captain would be the captain of my yard, Facility D.

In another occasion, I was approached by Lieutenant Jeffrey Brown and Captain Williams in the Program Office, at which time Lieutenant Brown jokingly yelled out to me that he had the FBI on the phone and asked who I had told on now. I expected Captain Williams to reprimand him; his remark was highly unprofessional, not to mention the sensitivity and seriousness of the issue. The captain did nothing. In yet another incident, I was on the yard passing by Williams and Brown when Lieutenant Brown yelled out that I was a rat and asked what authorities I was going to call next.

Later that same day, on the yard with the yard sergeant and other officers, I heard the alarms start to yelp from Housing Unit 3. The other officers and I ran across the yard to answer the call. As I approached, the outside door to the unit was wide open; I didn't hesitate to run right in. More than a dozen inmates were engaged in an all-out brawl; they were swinging broom sticks, mop handles, and anything else they could get there hands on. I turned around expecting to see the back up I had arrived with. No one; not a single officer had entered the unit with me.

A part of me wanted to panic—was I being set up for a hit, left to be attacked by a gang of heated inmates? As the only officer in there, I was an easy target. Luckily, using my pepper spray and handcuffs, I was able to get the situation under control.

When my "back up" finally entered, they said they had all stopped at the front door with the pathetic excuse that they were waiting for the yard sergeant to respond. I called bullshit. That was not CDC policy and they knew it. I was floored; there was no way I was gong to stand for that deliberate betrayal. I told the sergeant he could take my job and shove it up his ass.

That was my last day at Pleasant Valley State Prison.

CHAPTER THIRTEEN

NO TURNING BACK

After the events that had taken place at Pleasant Valley Prison I knew my life as a correctional officer was over. It didn't matter where I transferred, my story was exposed and I was labeled a traitor.

I sought help from Union President Mike Jimenez. After several of my phone calls and messages went unanswered, I made my way down to his office. When I found him, I mentioned I had been trying to get in touch with him and told him I needed help. To my dismay, he responded that he has been advised not to talk to me and began to walk away. I was stunned. I stopped him and told him the union was there for *us*, I had been paying my union dues for over thirteen years and this was the first time I have ever called on the union for help. He said that I needed to seek my own legal advice and continued to walk away.

Once again I was left in hysterics. A long-time friend of mine, Mark Hiepler, was an attorney, so I called him for legal advice. He referred me to attorney Lanny Tron—Lanny would later represent me in my civil case against the California Department of Corrections. Two weeks later I received a call from Lanny asking me to drive down to his office to meet with him. He stated that he had an important document from a confidential source in Sacramento and he wanted to share it with me. When I asked why he couldn't simply tell me over the phone, he said he did not want to exchange any information over the phone just in case the wires were tapped.

Upon arrival to his law office, Lanny asked if I thought I had been followed. We were on the same page; I had checked my rear view mirror constantly the entire drive down to Camarillo. Lanny was fearful of my case because it involved so many powerful people in the state government.

Our meeting started off by Lanny telling me he received a document in the mail without a return address on it, but the stamp was from Sacramento, California. It was a report from the Office of the Inspector General regarding the investigation into allegations concerning the Green Wall at Salinas Valley State Prison. There was a case number of *OIG 01-0177-CA*, followed by a summary of findings and conclusions. For the first time, I was hopeful; this was great for our case. The document was a four page report that took two years to complete before the Office of the Inspector General forwarded a copy to the director of the Department of Corrections for appropriate action on January 31, 2003.

Office of the Inspector General
Case # OIG 01-0177-CA

Background

On September 6, 2001, the Office of the Inspector General received an anonymous telephoned complaint alleging the existence of a "gang" of correctional officers at Salinas Valley State Prison known as the 7/23 or Green Wall. The complaint alleged that the group sets up inmates for assault by other inmates by revealing confidential "R" suffix information and that one member of the group, an Investigative Service Unit officer carries a weapon in his pant leg to plant on inmates. The complaint also alleged that the officers carry key chains and other items engraved with "7/23", possess photographs depicting banners with the words 7/23 and Green Wall, adhere to a Code of Silence, and threaten others with retaliation for challenging them. In the complaint it also alleges that the Salinas Valley State Prison warden alerts the group whenever the Office of Investigative Services is scheduled to conduct an investigation so that Green Wall contraband can be hidden.

In a separate complaint, filed in a September 24, 2001 memorandum, a Salinas Valley State Prison staff member claimed that s/he had been retaliated against for reporting alleged felony misconduct by Salinas Valley State Prison investigative services unit officers to the Salinas valley State Prison warden. The complainant also alleged that a vehicle belonging to another staff member had been vandalized at the prison after the owner sustained misconduct allegations against an investigative services unit officer.

During the course of the investigation, a lieutenant told the Office of the Inspector General that when s/he was assigned as the Investigative Services Unit lieutenant in 2001, s/he conducted a supervisory review of the unit's performance and discovered that several officers in the unit were under investigation for use-of-force incidents and other alleged misconduct. The lieutenant said s/he also found that officers assigned to the Investigative Services Unit had attempted to intimidate other members of the staff by placing a box of green pens on a desk with a sign reading, "Take one if you dare," and by making verbal statements that the warden wanted Investigative Services Unit officers to "go out and instill fear and intimidation in the inmates." In addition, it was alleged that certain correctional officers had tattooed themselves with "7/23", wore green wristbands, and signed official documents in green ink. The warden was reportedly informed of these matters, but took little or no action in response.

In 1999, the office of Investigative Services conducted an earlier investigation into allegations concerning the Green Wall group. That investigation found evidence that the facility had been vandalized with the numbers "7/23" and the letters "GW" marked on walls with marking pen and engraved into wet cement. A sheet of paper with a green Wall logo, consisting of a pair of dice and an upside-down horseshoe with the numbers 7 and 23, along with the satanic symbol "666," had also been found taped to the inside of a control room window. In the course of that investigation, officers admitted the existence of the Green Wall, but characterized its activities as simply officer "camaraderie."

The Office of the Inspector General conducted an extensive investigation into the allegations between October 2001 and May 2002. The investigation included interviews with twenty-five employees of Salinas Valley State Prison and with the Monterey County District Attorney.

In addition, the Office of the Inspector General reviewed numerous official reports and documents, including the original interviews from the 1999 Office of Investigative Services report, which sustained the existence of the Green Wall group. The Office of the Inspector General also reviewed a number of Investigative Services Unit reports and other relevant documents and photographs and collected evidence that included two knives, a green knife engraved with "7/23," and a smaller black-handled pocket-knife.

Findings and Conclusions

As a result of the investigation, the Office of the Inspector General confirmed several of the allegations concerning the Green Wall group, including allegations covered in the earlier Office of Investigative Services investigation. Specifically, the investigation determined the following:

A group of correctional officers at Salinas Valley State Prison formed an alliance in 1999 called the "Green Wall," or "7/23", representing the seventh and twenty-third letters of the alphabet, G and W.

Numerous incidents involving the Green Wall group took place at Salinas Valley State Prison between 1999 and 2001, including the vandalizing of institution property with "7/23" and "G/W" markings and taping on a window of a paper containing the Green Wall logo and the satanic symbol "666". The investigation confirmed that in May 2001 Investigative Services officers brought a green knife with "7/23" engraved on the handle into the facility as a promotion gift for an Investigative Services Unit sergeant. The investigation determined that the institution management did not properly control or investigate the incidents.

According to Salinas Valley State Prison managers, the warden maintained a relationship with several of the officers assigned to the Investigative Services Unit Security Squad that differed from his relationship with other members of the staff and may have influenced his actions in relation to those officers. The warden kept the Employee Relations officer and other managers "out of the loop" regarding misconduct investigations and disciplinary issues involving certain members of the Investigative Services Unit Security Squad. The evidence suggests that several members of the Investigative Services Unit belonged to the Green Wall group.

Over a period of approximately three months, from March to May 2001, the warden was repeatedly advised by several mangers about personnel problems in the Investigative Services Unit, but failed to take appropriate action in response to those reports.

The warden did not act on a correctional lieutenant's report that Investigative Services Unit officers might be involved in the Green Wall group and did not act on the lieutenant's request that the officers be temporarily reassigned to other duties while investigations concerning excessive force and other allegations of misconduct were pending against them.

No evidence was presented to support the allegations that officers promoted a "code of silence" or that they intentionally leaked confidential inmate information to other inmates for the purpose of causing assaults against those inmates. Similarly, insufficient evidence was presented to establish that members of the Green Wall group vandalized the vehicles of other staff members.

No evidence was presented to substantiate the allegation that the warden told officers when the Office of Investigative Service investigators were scheduled to arrive to conduct interviews.

In an interview with the Office of the Inspector General, the Salinas Valley State Prison warden was evasive, repeatedly answering questions about relevant events with "I can't recall," "I don't recall," and "possibly," and by otherwise providing non-meaningful responses. The warden asserted that the Monterey County District Attorney's Office had conducted a criminal investigation concerning the Green Wall, but that assertion was denied by the District Attorney's Office.

The warden admitted to knowing about the existence of the Green Wall group; he took no immediate action to discover what it was or who was involved and was slow to react to events at the prison involving officers assigned to the Investigative Services Unit Security Squad. The warden's unwillingness or inability to take action to identify and correct the Green Wall situation led to lapses in communication between supervisors/managers and line-level staff.

The situation fostered an atmosphere of distrust and prevents a timely investigation and resolution of allegations concerning employee misconduct.

When I finished reading the report, I didn't know if I wanted to cry or scream out loud. All along I was telling the truth about the "Green Wall." I wasn't "ratting" anyone out, officers were involved in illegal activities and when I was asked about the situation, I had the courage to stand up and tell the truth.

Lanny told me that this was a great piece of evidence for the case. Further, it was evidence against the California Department of Corrections, that they made no effort to protect me from my written disclosure—making me an outcast. Lanny said I was a true whistleblower and we had an upward battle that was just getting started. Before leaving his office, Lanny warned me to watch my back, carry my weapon and to always wear my bullet proof vest.

CHAPTER FOURTEEN

THE CONFRONTATION

I picked my son up from my ex-wife's home and intended on spending some much needed quality time with him. Needing a break myself, I brought him with me to visit my parents, who were staying by the beach. It was a warm summer evening on July 29, 2003. Daulton, who was now eight years old, and I went to the Mid-State Fair in Paso Robles, California. The Mid-State Fair was a huge attraction, drawing big-name stars like Toby Keith, Kenney Chesney, Steely Dan, and Alan Jackson. That day, I must have gone on every ride. Daulton held my hand, leading me from one ride to the next. A few times, I thought I was going to be sick, but seeing all the fun he was having, I couldn't stop. I let him lead me from one rollercoaster to the next and I enjoyed every minute of it.

At about eleven o'clock that night, the day's excitement had worn Daulton out. As we were leaving the fair hand-in-hand, just passing thought the main gate, I heard someone yell my name.

"Hey, Vodicka!"

I turned and recognized Correctional Sergeant James George and a woman sitting on a bench. I stepped towards Sergeant George to exchange a friendly handshake, when all of a sudden Sergeant George leaped from the bench. Catching me off guard, he yelled, demanding to know if I was suing Officer Archibald.

I felt my son's hand clench tightly down on mine. I moved forward and put myself between George and Daulton. I told George I could not talk about the matter. He then waved his hand towards my face with a closed fist and in a threatening tone, repeatedly told me that I had to drop the case. People began to take notice of the confrontation. George went on to shout that Archibald was a close friend of his and that I needed to back off and let it go. Daulton pulled down on my hand telling me he was scared. That was it; I immediately placed my hand onto my concealed weapon and rushed towards my vehicle. I got Daulton in as quickly as possible and took off.

After the encounter with Sergeant George, I began to experience more anxiety and emotional distress. I now not only feared for my own safety, but for the safety of those around me, especially my son. The next morning I called Lanny and advised him of the situation at the fair. Lanny informed me that Sergeant George was under violation of the law—for intimidating and/or threatening a witness—and that he would make certain he would be punished for his actions. Lanny then told me it would be a good idea for me to go into hiding.

Our trip was cut short. I immediately checked out of the hotel we were staying at, drove over to my parents and informed them about what had occurred the night before. We said our good-byes, my parents giving Daulton the traditional fifty-dollar bill to "buy whatever he wanted".

"Bye Grandma!"

"No, no. Until we meet again," she said.

In the car, Daulton was sleeping, so I took the time to call Lanny again. I guess in that short period of time, he did some research and found Sergeant George was under violation of *Penal Code 136.1*, which states:

> *136.1. (a) Except as provided in subdivision (c), any person who does any of the following is guilty of a public offense and shall be punished by imprisonment in a county jail for not more than one year or in the state prison:*
>
> *(1) Knowingly and maliciously prevents or dissuades any witness or victim from attending or given testimony at any trial, proceeding, or inquiry authorized by law.*
>
> *(2) Knowingly and maliciously attempts to prevent or dissuade any witness or victim from attending or giving testimony at any trial, proceeding, or inquiry authorized by law.*

He continued to say George had even broke California Government Code 8547.2, which states:

> *(b) In pertinent part, that an improper governmental activity means any activity by a state agency or by an employee that is undertaken in the performance of the employee's official duties, and that is in violation of any state or federal law or regulation.*

Lanny filed a complaint to the State Personnel Board of Control, Government Claims Branch; six months later, on January 28, 2004, it was finally reviewed. Soon after, I received a call from Lanny saying he had just received a letter from the State Personnel Board; the incident with Sergeant George was scheduled for a hearing next year, on June 8, 2005 in Salinas, California.

CHAPTER FIFTEEN

SENATE TESTIMONY

"Can the California Department of Corrections police itself? The answer, I believe, is no. But starting today it must. California's prison system teeters on the brink of being declared bankrupt, not only in its policy but in its morality, starting with top prison brass. It is one judge's order away from being pulled into receivership and run by a federal court. It is a tarnished institution. The California Department of Corrections has lost its ability and integrity to police itself. Structural reform from the top to the bottom is mandated. But even the best of reforms can be merely relegated to paper. It's the people and their elected or appointed leaders who give meaning and realization to the value of the piece of paper on which any policy is written. We don't just need a review and overhaul of the policy; we need a review and overhaul of the people who are charged with running one of the nation's largest prison system. If top officials neither understand nor care about the need for fair investigations, they are unlikely to investigate thoroughly and without prejudice or to impose discipline when thing go wrong. California's prison directorate has far too often chosen to look the other way in dealing with problems of officer misconduct and investigative services. We have seen them shut down investigations, including submitting false documents to a court. There are systemic problems in the CDC that top brass have not only ignored but become accomplices to sanctioning a "Code of Silence" at the highest level of government. And now, California's top brass are facing possible charges of contempt of court and perjury. This is an outrage."

This was Senator Gloria Romero's opening statement before my testimony during the Senate Select Committee on Government Oversight on January 20, 2004.

Senator Jackie Speier's opening statement was just as powerful. "Today's hearing is the fourth in a series of hearings that the Select Committee on

Government Oversight and the Select Committee on the California Correctional System have had over the course of two years and two administrations. Last year, during the course of our hearings, there was a statement made by a man that goes like this: 'No two women are going to tell me how to run the prisons.' Now, Mr. Alameida, Senator Romero and I don't want to be wardens. We just want justice done. We want the men and women who run the nation's largest correctional system to honor the public trust that has been placed in their hands."

Senator Speier continued, "Much of the testimony we will hear today will be startling and even unbelievable. Whistleblowers who speak under oath fear for their jobs and their lives. Our next topic is Salinas Valley State Prison and the "Green Wall." We're going to hear now from Correctional Officer Donald Vodicka."

"Come on," said Lanny, "We're up."

During the testimony I gave precise details about the "Green Wall" and how the warden's office had intentionally leaked my confidential report to other staff members.

Senator Romero then stated, "You indicated that you believe that the report, and then subsequent to that, that others were leaked because you began to get the—basically, being ostracized by other officers you began to be intimidated. At one point, I understand from your court brief, that you were threatened, as well yourself, and I believe your child?"

"That's a hard subject," I replied.

"Thank you Officer Vodicka. I won't ask further. I do have it in writing and I'll go ahead, and that will be part of the testimony overall," she said.

"I can answer that. Just give me a minute."

Lanny put his hand on my shoulder and whispered in my ear, "Are you alright? You can stop if you want."

I told him I would continue with the questions from Senator Romero.

I pulled myself up to the microphone, "In July, I'm not going to tell you where I live, because I still currently live in that area—because I fear for my safety right now. And both Senators, I'm wearing a protective bulletproof vest on me right now. I want to put that on record. I was attending a fair and my little boy was with me. As I was leaving the fairgrounds, I was approached by a supervisor that I knew at the institution. As I was walking out, he yelled at me, 'Hey, Vodicka!' I go 'Hey, how you doing?' I walked over to him, shook his hand. Right away he stood up and says, 'Are you suing so and so?' I said, 'I can't talk about it.' And he says, 'You need to back off.' And he started yelling, 'Back off! Let it go! He's a friend of mine.' My little boy got startled. He goes, 'Dad, what happened?' I didn't want to tell him; he's only eight years old. He doesn't live in California. We both then walked immediately to my vehicle. I contacted my attorney immediately the next morning and followed up with several reports with no prevail."

Senator Romero began, "This will be an issue that certainly we're going to raise tomorrow in terms of when we do reports and we receive reports, who receives them? Should they remain under seal? Who should receive them? That will be subject to tomorrow's testimony. Mr. Rimmer, let me ask you some questions here. What steps are taken to protect an officer who has been asked— no, let me correct that, who has been directed, *ordered*, by his superior to write a report on something like the "Green Wall?" The officer writes the report, submits it to his superiors. What is supposed to happen in terms of protection of that officer from any potential negative fallout, as has been described by Officer Vodicka?"

Mr. Rimmer was seated to the right of me. He was the acting Director of Corrections at the time—the former Director of Corrections Mr. Edward Alameida had been relieved from his duties.

Mr. Rimmer responded, "Well, it really depends on the specifics of the particular case, and each case is going to vary a little bit from—it could be anything as simple as keeping the information confidential with only restricted copies, restricted reading, of whatever the information may be, up to and including a security detail on that particular individual. It could include a change of job assignment."

Senator Romero stated, "Well he was changed. If we expect individuals to step forward to break the Code of Silence or the 'code of cowardice,' do you think that we have sufficient protections and reassurances for officers today that when they step forward, that what occurred to Officer Vodicka will not happen to them?"

Senator Romero was getting very upset; Mr. Rimmer was clearly trying to dance around the questions.

He responded, "I think we need to do some rebuilding within the department to ensure that all staff is protected from any kind of work environment that even closely resembles this. Its applicable not only in the institution but throughout the department and basically, all of our facilities. And I think we have some work to do in that regard."

Calmer now, Senator Romero said, "I agree with you that we do have work to do. It sounds like, from the description from what I've read, he stepped forward, he did the right thing; he did what he was ordered to do. He followed his professional duties. He submitted his reports with the belief and the understanding that these would be confidential; that appropriate individuals would receive them. Nothing appeared to be done when it was learned that this material had been leaked or exposed to folks who were outside the chain of who should receive it. He was transferred. It sounds like harassment and intimidation occurred there as well, to the point of having a child witness a confrontation. Yeah, I think we do have some work to do, and my hope would be that when we—as I heard Secretary Hickman express this morning, he does not condone the Code of Silence; he will be active against a Code of Silence. But as we do so, let it be understood that to do so, we're going to have to still, probably, provide some protections that right now are missing."

Senator Speier began, "Let me ask you further, Mr. Rimmer. You know, to me, the worst thing that can happen to a correctional peace officer, one of the worst things that can happen, is to do what he's been asked to do or come forward with information as a whistleblower and then have others become aware of it and then have his reputation, credibility, safety, compromised by comments made by other correctional officers that he's a snitch. What regulation, what protocol, exists within the department to take adverse action against individuals who jeopardize the safety of individuals who come forward as whistleblowers?"

Rimmer looked dumbfounded, "Well, I think in this particular instance, and maybe Mr. Hoshino can elaborate for me, there was action taken regarding some of the events that Mr. Vodicka spoke to."

Mr. Hoshino was in charge of all the Office of Investigations Services and answered to the Director of Corrections, who was Mr. Rimmer at the time. Senator Speier leaned as far as she could without leaving her chair as she directed her question to Mr. Rimmer. She was going to give it to him now for pawning the question off to Mr. Hoshino.

"Well you know, I don't think that's really a very good answer. Let's not talk about Mr. Vodicka for a minute. I've got the copy of the Inspector's General's report, which doesn't say a whole lot. What do you normally do? If I come forward and give you information that is incriminating to another officer but I'm a whistleblower and that gets out on the yard and I'm starting—I'm called a snitch—that's like having, you know a red target placed on your head for inmates to come after you and for other correctional officers not to support you if there is, in fact, some scuffle. So, what do you do presently?"

Mr. Hoshino began, "Senator, if I may. I know this is a sore subject for me to rise with folks, but this is a department-wide problem. This is a problem that we're trying to address. It has to do with confidentiality, protecting people's identity. It appears to me that Officer Vodicka was directed to submit information and that information went to an investigative unit. That investigative unit has certain responsibilities with that information and they didn't take care of their responsibilities with that information. It's the same responsibilities that we're trying to take care of in OIS. In fact, it's not just in those places; it's department-wide. There is too much information and too much identity about investigations and individuals who are stepping forward that are just getting out and getting around inappropriately, and it compromises the individuals and it compromises the investigations."

Senator Speier stated, "You're stating a fact in evidence, but what are we doing about the 'Lieutenant Browns' who make the statements, 'You're a snitch' and jeopardize the safety of another officer? You're not going to stop this at all if the people who call the whistleblowers, snitches, aren't reprimanded."

"I agree with that Senator," said Mr. Hoshino.

"But meanwhile, we have whistleblowers whose lives are being destroyed. So, there is no policy about going after individuals who make statements about officers being snitches because they've gotten word that they are, in fact, whistleblowers?"

Mr. Hoshino was crouching very low in his seat, "Not that I know of and not that I have uncovered in the ninety days that I've been there."

"That, to me, is probably one of the most outrageous things we've heard today. Let me ask you this, based on hearing Mr. Vodicka's explanation of what happened, what should have happened Mr. Rimmer?"

Ms. Keeshen, Department of Corrections Senior Legal Staff, interrupted, "Excuse me, Senator. I hate to butt in. As the department's legal advisor, I have communicated the fact that this matter was going to be on calendar today to our litigation counsels at the Office of the Attorney General's Office. They advised us not to communicate the particulars with respect to this case as it is an active litigation."

Lanny became furious with this statement. He stood up from his chair. "Senators, I think that's the whole problem. This has been going on since 2001. We tried everything. We wrote to Alameida, Duncan, and the wardens, 'Help him out. Help him out! Do something for him.' Nothing. We wrote to Gray Davis. Nothing. 'Have the IG take a look at it.' Now he walks around with a bulletproof vest. That can't be right, okay? An excuse of what's an active litigation, it should never get there! He's a state employee. He should never have been here."

Next to Mr. Rimmer, was Cheryl Pliler, second in charge of the Department of Corrections.

Ms. Pliler stated to the Senators, "Maybe I've been blessed in my career, but I have never heard some of the stories like I've heard today, and that covers thirteen different assignments. However, I will tell you that what I've heard today is not acceptable conduct by the Department of Corrections' employees. There is regulatory law currently in place that says you will respect your fellow employees; you will not be discourteous to fellow employees. And there's Government Code regulation as well."

Senator Romero then asked Ms. Pliler, "What about, you will not endanger your fellow employees?"

Ms. Pliler leaned forward, "You will not speak about personal and confidential information regarding other employees."

Senator Romero then asked her, "Are there disciplinary actions taken when that is reported?"

"Absolutely," Ms. Pliler quickly answered.

Romero then asked, "Why didn't it happen in this case?"

Pliler, acting dumb-founded stated, "I can't answer about this case. I don't know. I'm not up on the history with this particular case, but I have taken discipline myself on employees who became not to this level of treatment of other employees but for discourteous treatment of other employees."

"I know we're in litigation. We're not here to try the lawsuit, but again, too, I would agree with you - we shouldn't have to be here," said Senator Romero.

Senator Romero continued, "The whole point is that if there was a procedure in place, if there were policies that were clear and understood, if there was training, and if there was the backbone and the willingness to speak out, it would seem to me that we wouldn't have to be sitting in a committee hearing being advised by our legal counsel, 'Don't talk about it; it's the subject of litigation.' Money we're spending to resolve lawsuits that seem to me, unnecessary, could be going into training of officers and putting forth, really, what we should be doing in the Department of Corrections."

Senator Speier turned towards me, "Mr., Vodicka, thank you very much for your testimony here today. I have one last question. Do you want to return to work at the Department of Corrections?"

"I can't. I can't, it'll follow me where ever I go," I said.

"Well, that's what we've got to change in the department," said Senator Speier.

At the conclusion of my testimony, I exited the State Capitol where I was bombarded by the media. Lanny slipped his business card to the acting Director of Corrections, Richard Rimmer, and told him that I needed twenty-four-hour protection. Rimmer assigned it to the Special Services Unit, who would look into the matter to see if it was valid for me to be protected after my testimony.

Together, Lanny, Joe Reynoso and I rushed to my car. I said good bye to my friend Joe.

"Biggen, watch out for yourself at all times, you did the right thing and you will prevail, call me everyday so I know you're safe." Reynoso said.

Lanny and I headed to Sacramento Airport, where I dropped him off.

"I am proud of you man, you did the right thing and I am with you until the end."

He then told me, not to return to my residence, to get out of the state of California.

"BRIDGE LEADING TO HIDE OUT"

"LOCKED GATE LEADING TO HIDEOUT"

"LONELY DIRT ROAD TO HIDEOUT"

"HIDEOUT HOUSE"

"SNOW TRACTOR"

Chapter Sixteen

The Hideout

It was a dark, foggy drive heading north on Interstate 5. I headed to the mountains, where the air was clear and I would be safe—isolated, away from the public. I arrived in a small town called Dunsmuir and stopped at a run-down motel at the end of town. I was exhausted from the emotional day of testifying, I just needed a hot shower and a warm bed.

The next morning I woke up to a train whistle. On my hunt for fresh coffee, I thought to myself what a beautiful area Dunsmuir was to live; to live away from prisons and the crowds. The town was surrounded by giant redwood trees and in the distance you could hear water running down the streams. If I stayed here, maybe no one would know who I was; I could start over. Later, I toured the town, looking for a place to stay.

Luckily, not to long into my search, in the second floor window of a quaint house, I saw a *For Rent* sign.

The owner had a welcoming smile on her face and she introduced herself as Mary Ann. The unit was very well kept; it had hardwood floors, a sufficient living room, a full kitchen, a bathroom, and a bedroom large enough to fit a queen size bed. It was perfect. The rent was four hundred dollars a month, including utilities.

After friendly chatter, she asked me what kind of work I did. Although I felt oddly close to my new landlord, I didn't want to get into the whole story. I told her that I was a correctional officer at a state prison in California, and that I was on medical leave.

I was shocked when one day I read in the newspaper, that an inmate from Salinas Valley State Prison sent Senator Romero a letter with a white powdery substance inside the envelope along with a letter:

> *You better back off with the investigation of the Green Wall or we*
> *will kill you and your family.*

The entire state and the Department of Corrections were in an uproar. They sent a team of investigators to the prison and thought they discovered the inmate who sent the death threat. They interviewed him for hours, he took a lie detector, which he passed; he was found innocent and not charged. Attention was then turned toward prison staff. *Well duh,* I thought. *What business would an inmate have, trying to stop an investigation of the Green Wall? If anything, they would be on justice's side.*

A couple of days had past when I received a phone call from Lanny.

"Fox News wants to do an interview with you here in Los Angeles. They want you to tell your story on television, to the world."

"Ok, when is this supposed to happen?"

"They want to do it on Friday."

We were picked up at Lanny's office and driven to Fox's satellite station in Santa Monica, California. I was extremely nervous as Lanny and I were being hooked up with microphones. The famous Gibson and Heather Naurett conducted the five-minute live interview about The "Green Wall" inside Salinas Valley State Prison. After the interview, the media frenzy really took off. Several time a day, reporters contacted Lanny, wanting to set up an interview with me.

Shortly after the interview, Lanny received a phone call from a high ranking official in the Department of Corrections, requesting to meet with him in Sacramento. Lanny flew up for the meeting, where he was handed a document and told that it should help out greatly with our lawsuit. It was a copy of a Corrective Action Plan by the California Department of Corrections concerning the "Green Wall." (For privacy reasons, the official who provided us with the document will remain anonymous.) Lanny made copies of the document and placed them into an envelope and mailed one to his office in Camarillo before boarding the long flight back to Ventura County. Lanny told me that he wanted a copy sent in the mail, just in case something went wrong flying home.

Lanny asked me, "Where can I send this document to you?"

"Send it to this address, attention Mary Ann..."

The next day I went to the Post Office with Mary Ann to pick up the document. By this time, I had informed her of my situation. She told me she had a better place for me to stay, somewhere safer and even more isolated than Dunsmuir.

We loaded up both of her dogs—Boogie and Betsy—into the back of the truck. Boogie was a mix, part wolf and German Sheppard, and Betsy was a cute little mutt. Mary Ann said that Boogie wasn't afraid of anything and could hear someone coming from miles away. Boogie was my new best friend.

We turned off the freeway onto a single-lane paved road through the giant redwoods following the river alongside of us. We climbed up the side of the mountain until we arrived at a locked gate. Mary Ann unlocked the gate and we continued to drive for another five miles. Finally we arrived to her secret place; two cabins sat on the property, hugging the stream. They had no electricity, no cable and no phones. Mary Ann's cabin was closest; the second cabin was about half of a mile back, that would be my cabin.

I headed for my new hideout, anxious to check it out. I also wanted to sit alone and read the document Lanny had mailed. Boogie followed close behind me.

I opened the envelope, the cover page was dated April 15, 2004; about three months after I testified. The subject line was in bold letters and read:

CORRECTIVE ACTION PLAN – OFFICE OF THE INSPECTOR GENERAL'S REPORTS RELATED TO THE "GREEN WALL" AND "CODE OF SILENCE" AT SALINAS VALLEY STATE PRISON

The second document that was also in the envelop that was attached to the Corrective Action Plan and was signed by the acting Director of Corrections, Richard Rimmer, and Agent Secretary, Roderick Q. Hickman, who answered to the governor—Arnold Schwarznegger was signed by the acting Director of Corrections, Richard Rimmer, and the Agency Secretary, Roderick Q. Hickman, who answered to the governor—Arnold Schwarzenegger.

Memorandum

February 17, 2004

To: All California Department of Corrections Employees.

ZERO TOLERANCE REGARDING THE "CODE OF SILENCE"

The California Department of Corrections (CDC) is only as strong as the values held by each of its employees, sworn and non-sworn. How we conduct ourselves inside our institutions and in the Central Office is a reflection of those values.

The "Code of Silence" operates to conceal wrongdoing. One employee, operating alone, can foster a Code of Silence. The Code of Silence also arises because of a conspiracy among staff to fail to report violations of policy, or to retaliate against those employees who report wrongdoing. Fostering the Code of Silence includes the failure to act when there is an ethical and professional obligation to do so.

Every time a correctional employee decides not to report wrongdoing, he or she harms our Department and each one of us by violating the public's trust. As members of law enforcement, all Correctional officers must remain beyond reproach. The public's trust in this Department is also violated by retaliating against, ostracizing, or in anyway undermining those employees who report wrongdoing and/or cooperate during investigations. There is no excuse for fostering a Code of Silence.

Your hard fought efforts to protect the public deserve recognition. Recently, however, the public's trust has been undermined by the operation of a Code of Silence within the CDC. To correct this problem we are taking steps to ensure the Department exemplifies integrity and instills pride. Part of this effort is the immediate implementation of a zero tolerance policy concerning the Code of Silence. We will not tolerate any form of silence as it pertains to misconduct, unethical, or illegal behavior. We also will not tolerate any form of reprisal against employees who report misconduct or unethical behavior, including their stigmatization or isolation.

Each employee is responsible for reporting conduct that violates Department policy. Each supervisor and manger is responsible for creating an environment conducive to these goals. Supervisors are responsible for acquiring information and immediately conveying it to managers. Managers are responsible for taking all appropriate steps upon receipt of such information, including initiating investigations and promptly disciplining all employees who violate departmental policy.

Any employee, regards of rank, sworn or non-sworn, who fails to report violations of policy or who acts in a manner that fosters the Code of Silence, shall be subject to discipline up to and including termination.

The Corrective Action Plan written by the Warden at Salinas Valley State Prison read as follows.

Pursuant to your direction, I have prepared a Corrective Action Plan to address the issues raised by the Office of the Inspector General (OIG) in their investigations about the existence of the Green Wall and prevalence of a Code of Silence among the staff at Salinas valley State Prison. Another major contributing factor to the climate of Salinas Valley was the management team. Since its activation Salinas Valley had seven wardens in a few years. Gary Lindsey, the first warden, retired approximately 18 months after activation and a string of interim wardens followed. It was not until 2000 when Anthony Lamarque was appointed, that Salinas Valley had some stable leadership from a warden.

One statement that was frequently repeated to supervisors and managers in a variety of staff meetings by Warden Lamarque was that, 'You run your yards; I am not going to make decisions for you. Each of you is responsible for your yard and what goes on there.' I think the degree of autonomy that this message conveyed coupled with a lack of management tools to audit operations and general lack of oversight created a climate ripe for abuse by staff. I was there when Lamarque was appointed in 2000, only then did staff began to hear a message that there was an administration in place whose goal was to establish and maintain a safe working environment, hold inmates accountable by the application of the disciplinary process and classification process and that staff were recognized as working in a tough environment. This was the first time that officers felt support by the warden.

However, there was a pattern of failures to establish and maintain staff accountability for their actions and send a clear message about expectations that officers comply with the law and conduct themselves professionally. This is when the officers took it upon themselves that they were supported and could engage in some level of misconduct without fear of consequences, otherwise known as the Green Wall.

Inherent in this subculture is a belief that they are duty bound to each other to protect each other's interests at all costs from any attack. Their sense of loyalty will therefore go to protecting a fellow member from any disciplinary action or criminal action by either passively or actively concealing evidence, withholding evidence, or outright dishonesty with investigators. The Code of Silence is an integral part of what is created by a Green Wall subculture. Having identified what I believe is the root causes of the "Green Wall" and the consequent "code of silence", a plan of action to correct and counter the negative culture has been formulated and implemented. The plan of attack is multifaceted and requires both a long-term commitment and absolute consistency in its execution.

Inherent in this plan is the need to identify strategies to address segments of the staff population with messages, expectations, training and actions tailored to their needs and designed to bring about cohesion.

Commencing on February 17, 2004, a 2-hour class on Ethics Training was developed and presented to all staff at Salinas Valley State Prison. The class was conducted by associate wardens, the acting chief deputy warden, and one facility captain. Two of the instructors had participated in the public safety leadership ethics training and are certified instructors.

This training included videotaped, approximately six minutes long, which communicated clear set values and ethical standards for conduct by all employees. The same oath administered at the academy for all peace officers in the Department of Corrections was read to participants and was an integral part of the ethic message.

Part of the ethics training included a power point presentation. There were a number of slides developed for this presentation that articulated a core set of values essentials for our profession. These values statement slides have been formatted into posters and have been distributed and posted throughout the administration building. Within the next few weeks, additional sets of the posters will be printed up and posted throughout the prison. This is part of the overall strategy to saturate the institution with a clear and unambiguous message about values and ethical standards.

The area of staff investigations is one of the most complex and sensitive issues confronting Salinas Valley in its mission to shed the "Green Wall" stigma, regain the public's confidence, and instill pride and ethical behavior among all staff. To properly outline the staff investigative role in the plan of attack requires a breakdown of a number of steps and considerations.

The investigative services unit has been the topic of a great deal of media attention surrounding the "Green Wall" incidents. No one who had any complicity in the "Green Wall" misconduct is assigned to the investigative services unit.

A complete overhaul of the tracking processes for staff investigations has been completed. A number of serious deficiencies were noted after I assumed the acting warden position, specifically the investigative log was audited and found to have numerous CAT II investigations overdue. Most disturbing was that the subjects of some of these investigations were close personal friends *of the warden. Contact was made with the Office of Internal Affairs and with the cooperation of Martin Hoshino, a team has been assigned to complete these investigations some which may be criminal.*

To insure that staff investigations received a high level of support that they require in order to convey a message to all staff that misconduct will not be tolerated, I have ensured that I am personally involved in supporting the investigative efforts. This includes actively supporting OIA, OIG, ISU, Monterey County sheriff's department and Monterey County District attorney's office. The level of personal involvement gets back to line staff very quickly with the message that "This management team is no joke."

Also in the Corrective Action Plan, I read what I had corroborated earlier:

On November 26, 1998 approximately 28 Hispanic inmates attacked staff on Facility D. Eighteen correctional staff members were injured, 14 of whom were treated at Salinas Valley Memorial Hospital in Salinas. This incident, SVP-FDY-98-11-0644, became popularly known as the Thanksgiving Day Riot. The staff who were involved in this riot, and other staff who had been involved in other such disturbances, began to wear enameled turkey pins on their uniforms. These turkey pins symbolized the staff's solidarity with each other and were worn as if it were a campaign medal from the military, awarded for participation in a combat action. According to some accounts this riot had the effect of galvanizing staff solidarity and staff's belief that they were engaged in essentially combat operations and hence may be the origin of the Green Wall.

Sometime during the period from November 26, 1998 to 2001 a number of acts and incidents were attributed to staff associated with the Green Wall. The acts included placing graffiti in staff spaces and offices, developing hand signals to show their association with the Green Wall, having their bodies tattooed with the numbers 7/23, placing license plates frames on their vehicles with the numbers 7/23 on them, and requesting home telephone numbers and cell phone numbers with the last four digits 0723. In addition, there were allegations of intimidation of inmates and staff by members of the Green Wall, as well as acts of violence. The most notable incident of violence attributed to the

> Green Wall involved four members of the Investigative Services
> Unit who, while conducting a cell search, used unnecessary and
> excessive force on an inmate.

It was also indicated in the report that there was evidence of various staff stonewalling investigators by either arranging their stories ahead of time or hedging their answers. One theme that became clear from reading these investigations and talking with staff was that line officers, sergeants and lieutenants, with the direct or tacit support of some mangers, viewed the inmate population as less than human and deserving of any retributive act that staff may impose on them given an opportunity to do so.

On May 7, 2004, I received an e-mail from Richard Steffen, who was Senator Speier's aide:

> Senator Speier asked the director to review your case. SB1342
> and SB1431, the two Speier bills, protect CDC Whistleblowers,
> are in the Appropriations Committee. SB 1431 requires CDC to
> specifically set up a protection program against Whistleblowers.
> We drafted this bill based on your case."

Governor Arnold Schwarzenegger later signed the bills in January 2005.

🛡 🛡 🛡

I received a phone call from Lanny on Valentine's Day; my deposition was scheduled for February 23, 2005, at the Monterey Peninsula Court Reporters in Monterey, California. It was scheduled to take place over a course of three days.

Not only was I surprised when Lanny informed me that the Deputy Attorney General and the Department of Corrections wanted to videotape my deposition, but the Deputy Attorney General also contacted the judge and demanded that I not wear my weapon during the deposition. The judge granted her motion.

The first day of my deposition was horrible. For reasons still unknown, the Deputy Attorney General went off on a crazed tangent and accused me off sexually molesting my son. Her ludicrous allegations enraged me. In her extremely repulsive attempt to push my buttons, I almost lost it—slamming my fists onto the wooden table so hard, I shattered the glass of water that was next to me. Lanny jumped from his chair, he was furious, telling her she was out of line and he wanted it stricken from the transcript

Lanny and I took a short break, giving me time to gather myself and cool off.

Outside, Lanny calmed me down, "You have to keep your composure. They are trying to see if they can push your buttons. They are going to dig up the worst shit on you and keep nailing you to try to show you lose control when under pressure."

I was prepared for that, I was not prepared to be accused of sick, unthinkable acts.

The next two days were a lot easier on me. We started from the very beginning, rehashing ever incident, every event, and every detail. They tried to trip me up on questions about The "Green Wall," but my story stayed the same. It's easy to remember the truth.

On my way back to Mary Ann and the cabins, I received a phone call from Lanny; he received a notice to appear in the Monterey County Civil Court on the following Monday and needed my presence there. Judge Fields wanted both sides to appear in front of him.

Mary Cain-Simon, the Deputy Attorney General representing the California Department of Corrections, was standing by the courtroom door when I arrived—she couldn't even look me in the eyes. The bailiff stepped out and asked us to enter the courtroom. Judge Fields wanted to know how the case was coming along. He also stated that he wanted to schedule a trial date within the next few months, before the end of the year.

As I was leaving the courtroom, the bailiff handed me a note.

> *Officer Vodicka I have a great deal of respect for what you have done, I take my hat off to you. I know what great danger you must be in.*

When I showed Lanny, he advised me not to lose it. Shortly after our meeting, Lanny informed Mary Cain-Simon that he was ready to start our depositions.

Chapter Seventeen

The Depositions

For the next few weeks, I spent time with my family in Arizona. The stress in my life was taking a toll on my mother's already declining health. One morning, I was sitting on the porch, when I received a phone call from Lanny. A film crew from the British Broadcasting Company in England contacted Lanny because they heard about my case and was anxious to tell my story; I agreed to interview with them. The interview was about the Green Wall, which later became a documentary called <u>America's Brutal Prisons.</u>

A week after the interview, Lanny told me that it was our turn to conduct depositions on the individuals that where involved in my case. I said good bye to my parents, worried if that was going to be the last time I saw my mother.

I picked up Lanny from his house and we started the long journey to Monterey, California. The drive was good for us; it cleared our heads as the thundering blue ocean pounded the shoreline next to us.

The deposition of
Edward Caden, Esq. Chief Deputy Warden (Ret), California Department of
Corrections

It was during the depositions, that I met retired Chief Deputy Warden Edward Caden. His demeanor was very professional and conclusive; a tall gentleman with grayish hair. When I looked at him, I felt that this man, who once was in charge of Salinas Valley State Prison, would provide us with some great evidence for my case. We sat around the conference table in a small office. The court reporter turned to Mr. Caden.

"Mr. Caden, you are to tell the truth, the whole truth, and nothing but the truth."

Caden replied, "Yes, I will."

"Do you know what the Green Wall is?" Lanny asked.

"Do I know what the Green Wall is?" Caden repeated.

"Yes."

"In the context of this, yes."

"What is that?"

Caden stated, "It is an alleged group of rogue officers who were engaged in intimidation of staff and intimidation of inmates—planting evidence and things of that nature. Allegedly this group also engaged in some—I guess I'd characterize it as sophomoric behavior by carving the initials GW or 7/23 in furniture or—you know, vandalizing, and things like that."

"Okay. We'll come to your experience as a warden at another time later in the deposition, and we can discuss this Green Wall some more. But let me just ask you one general question. At the time you were warden at Salinas Valley, did you ever look into the Green Wall?"

"I'm going to have to ask you to clarify that question."

Lanny asked, "What part was unclear?"

Caden replied back, "What part was unclear?"

"Were you ever asked to provide a Corrective Action Plan with respect to the Green Wall?"

"Yes."

"By whom?"

Caden stated, "George Galaza, the Regional Administrator in the Central Region."

"When did this take place and were you the warden at Salinas Valley during that time?"

"It's either the very end of January—I don't have that date clearly, but it was either the end of January or the beginning of February 2004. Somewhere in there."

"Okay."

Caden explained further, "I don't recall exactly what day Mr. Lamarque left and I assumed command."

Lanny asked, "Before taking on the job as chief deputy warden, had anyone discussed with you the allegations of the Green Wall at Salinas Valley State Prison? This is before you took on the job."

"Yes."

"By whom?"

"Anthony Lamarque," replied Caden.

"How many discussions?"

"It was one very brief discussion on May 8th, 2002. And it was at the end of the interview for the position."

"What do you recall that Mr. Lamarque said, and what did you say in reply?"

Caden stated, "…it was something to the effect, 'I got the IG on my butt about this Green wall thing. There is nothing to it. It's been investigated thoroughly. There is nothing to it.' I asked him, 'Well, what's this Green Wall thing?' And he says, 'Oh, it's just a bunch of b-s. Trust me. There is nothing to it.' And that was the extent of it. That was the conversation."

Yea, but you knew he was full of shit, I thought.

"After you arrived at Salinas Valley on Monday; did you have any further discussions with Mr. Lamarque about the Green Wall?"

"Yes, I did."

"How many?" Asked Lanny.

"I believe it was only one, one conversation. I asked Mr. Lamarque again, 'Tell me about this Green Wall. What's this about?' And he basically repeated to me that 'the Green Wall was this group of officers that are alleged to have been—you know—engaging in intimidation and this kind of behavior.' Again, he told me that, 'you know, it's been thoroughly investigated', and he basically rephrased what he had—I'm sorry—he repeated what he had said the previous time. The only thing that I asked was, 'Do you have any reports about this? Do you have any copies of the investigations?' To which he responded that he did not."

"He had no reports?"

"That's correct. That was what he told me. There were no reports at the institution about that investigation."

And the lies start to unravel, I thought to myself. *Lamarque lied to Caden— the OIG had previously investigated the Green Wall and found out there was in fact, a Green Wall gang that existed at the prison. Lamarque was fully aware of the rogue officers that he commanded.*

Lanny asked Caden, "Okay. Now, did you at some later date find that to be untrue? Were there reports at the institution about the Green Wall investigation?"

"Well, yes."

"When did you discover that?"

"Date is real hazy, but it would have been the end of January 2004."

"How is it that you discovered that to be untrue?" Lanny asked.

"This is a long answer. The day of a particular Senate hearing, I listened to the hearing on the Internet link, heard the testimony about Salinas Valley, heard some detailed information about the alleged Green Wall group. It seemed to be at odds with what I heard to that point. And I'm not taking as true what I'm hearing necessarily in front of the Senate, but it certainly raised some questions to me that I needed to resolve as the—essentially as the chief operating officer for that institution—as well as what was real and what's not. The next day I went in—this was over at my house on the grounds. I had some writing that I was trying to do that afternoon and just took off and went over there to do it. No phones.

And the next day when I went in—went into the office—that atmosphere was obviously very different. Mr. Lamarque's name had come up at the hearing. There was a report apparently introduced at the hearing from Steve White that was most uncomplimentary to Mr. Lamarque.

Lamarque and I had discussion in his office about this testimony. He was—he was quite concerned about the image that his institution was getting and you know—how he was being portrayed in the media. There was obviously media attention that followed right on the heels of that Senate hearing.

Lamarque was on the phone at some point—I believe it was that morning—with Central Region. I believe it was—who was on the phone— Tom Shanefelt, Steve Borg, and I think it's Ray Wilkins. He's a—those last two are both captains at Central Region.

Lamarque was asking them for a copy of the report that had been introduced at the Senate hearing related to him. I was in the office with him. So, I mean, he's saying this on his speakerphone in front of me. He was telling the folks on the phone that the former Regional Administrator, Ernie Roe, had promised him a copy of the report and the investigation and had never provided it. He said that over lunch. Don't people recall this? There was a lunch over there in Bakersfield. Jim Hamlet, Coordinate CTF, and Lamarque went to Bakersfield—had this lunch with Ernie Roe. Apparently Ernie had the report and back-up documents with it and was assigned to give Lamarque a copy. That was something like a year prior to that. And Lamarque was upset talking on the phone with him about the fact that he hadn't received it.

They promised then to send by fax as we were on the phone, a copy of this report, which they did. And Lamarque got it from the fax machine himself, made a photocopy of it, handed the photocopy to me to read. He read it. Well, after that, and after we were off the phone, I recall having a conversation with Tony. You know—this is an extremely damaging report. What's up with this? My impression was this Green Wall doesn't exist. This thing is saying something—certainly giving an impression that's very different from that.

I asked him again, 'Are there any investigative reports here at the institution related to this—anything related to this?' He says, 'I don't know at this point.'

I remember calling—calling somebody out in the Investigator Services Unit. I don't remember whether it was Captain Moore or Lieutenant Middlebrooks or somebody out there and said, 'I want you to bring any reports, any investigations related to the Green Wall back up to the warden's office now.'

I think it was about twenty minutes later; there were *eight file boxes* of material that were brought up to the office. I started reading through those boxes, and although they are—I'm not going to discuss the contents of the boxes because those are—those are privileged and would certainly be the subject of—but, nevertheless, there were things in there that gave me concerns about the existence of some group of nefarious little critters."

My reports were in those boxes, I thought.

Lanny asked Caden, "Did you ever have any discussions with anyone as to Vodicka's reports as to the Green Wall investigation?"

Caden replied, "In some very general terms, I remember Greg Lewis mentioning that Officer Vodicka had written some reports that were addressed to him. And, again, my recollection is that this was part of the dialogue that Lewis had with Lamarque, where Lamarque was not being responsive to it. And that was part of—you recall previously I was telling you about a conversation I was having with Greg Lewis. He was just kind of venting a little bit. He did tell me that there were documents involved in it, and looks like this may well have been some stuff that he was talking about.

Another high notoriety issue involves citizens' complaint, filed by myself. The complaint was sent to the warden's office and protested that Sergeant James George— then assigned to the Investigative Services Unit—approached Mr. Vodicka at the Paso Robles fair and threatened and intimidated him about a lawsuit he had filed against another employee and the department. No action was taken pursuant to the Penal Code to properly address this complaint. Upon learning of this issue, I took immediate steps to administratively reassign Sergeant James George from ISU, ensure that a formal investigation was instituted and I communicated directly with the attorney representing Mr. Vodicka giving him status of our efforts and my personal assurance that a thorough and fair investigation would be undertaken. This was addressed in the Corrective Action Plan—Office of the Inspector General's reports related to the Green Wall and Code of Silence"

When I met Mr. Edward Caden at our deposition, he was a man of integrity with a commitment to get the job done; an ethical individual who was committed to making positive changes at Salinas Valley State Prison. He emphasized to me that he conducted Ethics Training, based on my testimony in front of the Senators in Sacramento on the Green Wall at the prison.

At the deposition, Mr. Caden told me that he held a two-hour class that was developed for all staff at Salinas Valley State Prison, which focused on a clear set of values and ethical standards for conduct by all employees. At the conclusion, he gave strong warning to any staff member who was intent on violating the ethics of our profession. That if they do, they do so at their own peril and he has zero tolerance for deliberate misconduct. To this day, I have the utmost respect for Mr. Caden and what he did before retiring from the Department of Corrections.

The deposition of
Lieutenant Greg Lewis, California Department of Corrections

That same day, Lieutenant Greg Lewis was schedule for his deposition. This was the first time I had seen him in over three years. I was a bit confused when he did not greet me or shake my hand. We were friends; we lived in the same neighborhood, our families were close, and I was there for him when he was out of work due to an injury and through out his divorce. We had even kept in contact after he left Salinas Valley State Prison; I had no idea why there was such tension between us. I just hoped he would be truthful during his deposition.

Lanny began, "Do you recall receiving this document? First of all, do you recognize this document?"

I noticed Lewis had the same harsh look on his face that he always displayed when addressing someone.

"Yes," he answered.

"What is this document?"

Lewis stated, "This is a memorandum that I ordered Correctional Officer Vodicka to write, based upon his verbal report to me of this behavior."

I thought about that report he had me write about the Green Wall. *Greg, you where told by Lamarque to order me and my partner Gino to write a report of our knowledge of the Green Wall.*

"Did you discuss with him the contents of the documents?"

"I can't recall exactly, but I think it was one or two days prior to ordering him to write it."

"Where did you have the discussion?"

"In the investigative lieutenant's office—just myself and Officer Vodicka."

"How long was the meeting?"

"Maybe fifteen minutes."

I started to stew; this meeting *never* took place between me and Lewis, he wasn't telling the truth. *There was no meeting in your office! You took a golf cart and drove down to the Sally Port where Gino and I were working and you told both of us we had to write our reports and bring them to you.*

Lanny continued, "What was the meeting about to your recollection in the fifteen minute conversation."

Lewis stared right at me and I stared right back. *How could he be untruthful under oath?*

Lewis stated, "I remember Officer Vodicka relating that he had observed some behavior related to a group of officers that were associating themselves as the Green Wall."

"In your discussion, fifteen minutes or so with Officer Vodicka, did he describe the Code of Silence in addition to the Green Wall?"

"I can't recall the specific verbal conversation. I can recall him expressing concerns if the information was to be leaked out or disclosed that he would be subjected to retaliation by his peers."

"What was your reply to that concern, or did you have one?"

"I assured him that I would maintain this document as confidential and I personally handed this document to two special agents from the Office of Internal Affairs. I met with Warden Lamarque and requested an investigation, and part of the supporting documents that I requested was this memo."

Yeah right Greg, how else did the institution know about my report?

"Any allegations of the planting of contraband by staff associated with the Green Wall?"

"Only thing I can state was that an investigation was requested and initiated."

Come on Greg! You even told me that your evidence room officer advised you those members of the Green Wall entered the room and took several uncontrolled inmate-manufactured weapons from the locker without signing in, in the evidence room for entry. This was told to you by your evidence officer!

"Did you ever tell either Officer Negretti or Almauger that there had been—on one of the unit officer's desk—a box of green pens that said 'Take one if you dare'?" Lanny asked.

"Yes, I reported that to the warden. I recommended an investigation be initiated into some of the supporting facts. The documents that the green ink was utilized on were legal documents which are required to be signed in black ink."

"Now, you said you also reviewed investigative logs of the unit officers. Was there a number of unit officers that had disciplinary or misconduct investigations?"

"Yes."

"Did you ask Warden Lamarque to do something about these investigations?"

Lewis explained he had asked Lamarque, and that he requested the employees be reassigned from the unit until the investigations were completed. Lamarque denied Lewis' request. Lewis said he went back to the Investigative Services Unit and had a discussion with all the unit members and he spoke to them about his expectations of professionalism and following procedures. He said some staff responded with, "We're only doing what the warden has told us to do."

Lanny questioned further, "Did any correctional officer at Salinas Valley State Prison ever tell you that Warden Lamarque directed them to go out and install fear and intimidation into inmates?"

"Yes," answered Lewis.

"After the Vodicka handwritten memorandums, was there a time in which you were made aware of—what did they call this in here—'a green-handled buck knife engraved with 7/23 on it' being brought into the Salinas Valley State Prison?"

"All I can say is I met with Warden Lamarque and requested an investigation into misconduct by officers assigned to the Investigative Services Unit."

What the hell Greg! Why are you avoiding the full answers? You showed me the 989 Investigation Report that Lamarque refused to sign for an investigation… remember, it mentioned the officer's bringing the knife into the prison? This is ridiculous!

"Is the introduction of a knife into a prison a violation of California Penal Code?"

"Yes, it is," answered Lewis.

"Did you ever have a discussion with Officer Vodicka that an investigation into the Green Wall, 7/23 was not being followed up with a timely manner?"

"I do remember *a* discussion; I believe it took place after my attempt to initiate the investigation was denied by the warden."

Yeah Greg, it was at your house on Labor Day weekend. In fact, we had several discussions! I didn't understand why Lewis was being so vague and dishonest with Lanny. The thoughts were swirling around in my head. *What was Lewis hiding? Was someone telling him not to talk—threatening? Was he keeping his mouth shut so he can continue to climb up the latter to higher level position?* I thought Greg was better than this!

At the end of the deposition, we both stood up at the table and I reached my hand out to shake Lieutenant Lewis' hand. He stared at me for a moment, then quickly turned his back to me and headed for the door.

"He could have at least shaken your hand," Lanny said.

"I guess our friendship is over," I muttered.

*The deposition of
Correctional Officer Stephen Archibald, California Department of Corrections*

On the day of Archibald's deposition, it was about eight o'clock in the morning when in walked a petite lady—attorney Mary Cain-Simon and Officer

Archibald. I knew Archibald and I left on bad terms, but I offered my hand in greeting anyway; Archibald didn't even acknowledge the handshake.

He was sworn in by the court reporter, and then Lanny began.

"Have you ever had any discussions with Sergeant George about encounters Sergeant

George has had with Officer Vodicka?" Lanny asked.

"Yes," Archibald stated.

"How many discussions have you had about that encounter or an encounter?"

"Once or twice."

Here we go again! He was good friends with George and didn't speak with him "once or twice" like he claims.

"Once or twice? Do you recall when that was?"

"No. It was the time that—you know—he was removed from the squad for apparently a conflict he had with him at the fair grounds."

Bullshit Archibald! You and George car-pooled...you even told him that you were suppose to reveal all of your financial assets to the Attorney General for our testimony—which made you very scared...

"What was it that Sergeant George said was the conflict at the fairgrounds?"

"He said that—um—he shook his hand and told him that he should—um—you know, drop the suit with me, that I was a good guy, and that—you know—and apparently he got all upset about it and left the fair and later made—you know—false allegations which caused him to leave the squad. He actually, I guess, actually they were close because he actually pulled him to him and then said it to him. So it wasn't like they were yelling across at each other."

How would you know? You weren't even there!

I never thought Archibald had anything to do with the Green Wall, but after his deposition—the way he tried to cover for Sergeant George—it lead me to believe that maybe he did have some connections with the gang.

The deposition of
Internal Affairs Sergeant Azell Middlebrooks, California Department of
Corrections

After returning from lunch that same day, I noticed a short, stocky black man wearing a nice suit standing in a distance. I would recognize him from a mile away, I smiled—it was Sergeant Middlebrooks. I hadn't seen him in about three years. When we met, we greeted each other with a handshake and a friendly hug.

"Are you still at the prison?" I asked.

"Hell no, I am with OIA in Sacramento," Middlebrooks laughed.

We headed inside, with a smile Middlebrooks said, "Let's do this brother."

Azell sat right next to Mary Cain-Simon; she immediately whispered something in his ear—causing him to roll his eyes at me. Whatever she said to him, his facial expression told me he was not happy with what she had to say. The court reporter asked Azell to raise his right hand as she swore him for deposition testimony.

Lanny began the questioning, "Did you find Vodicka to be a credible individual?"

Middlebrooks responded, "Yes."

"Okay. To a squad officer, is it—I guess one of the most important traits— credibility?" "Yes sir."

"And if you lose your credibility, do you pretty much lose your ability to do an effective investigation?"

"I would say, as a peace officer, your credibility is questioned at all times."

"Have you ever seen a green-handled buck knife engraved with 723 on the blade?"

"Yes, I have. I saw it as a piece of evidence."

"Have you ever seen an invoice from a trophy shop in Salinas for the engraving of the 723 on the knife?"

Middelbrooks replied back, "Yes."

"Are you aware that a 989 had been signed for an investigation of the Green Wall at Salinas Valley State Prison?"

"Yes."

"Was the OIA and OIG investigating the Green Wall at Salinas Valley State Prison?"

"Yes."

Finally, someone tells the truth!

"Now, how long or how soon prior to Vodicka's leaving did you have the telephone call with Richard Ramsdell?"

"A few days. We spoke to each other. Basically we spoke regarding Mr. Vodicka and the fact that Mr. Ramsdell—I told him that I was familiar with Vodicka's problems at the institution and I would assist them in any way I could. I was also assisting them in trying to get him out of the institution to another location because of all the issues he was having at the institution. So we spoke about that. Mr. Ramsdell suggested that would be the best thing for the situation is to get Mr. Vodicka out of the institution. I concurred, and we did so."

At the conclusion of the deposition I walked outside with Azell where I thanked him for his honesty. We shared a heartfelt goodbye; this was the last time I ever saw Azell.

This was good day—it was the first time I felt comfortable being on the other end of the table. Hearing from Caden and Middlebrooks gave me hope—there *were* people within the Department of Corrections with ethics— man enough to come forward and tell the truth about the Green Wall.

That night, I asked Lanny who was up on hot seat tomorrow.

With a big smile on his face, he said, "Captain Moore and Sergeant Donnahoe."

The deposition of
Captain Miles Moore, California Department of Corrections

When we arrived for the depositions, I saw a black BMW sitting in the parking lot.

I told Lanny, "That's Captain Moore, sitting in his car staring at us."

Captain Moore was a tall black gentleman, about the size of me. He was in charge of the Investigative Services Unit and Internal Affairs at the prison, reporting to Warden Lamarque. It was nine o'clock in the morning when the court reporter swore Captain Moore in for the deposition. *This is going to be quite interesting…to watch him try to tell the truth*, I thought.

"If you could just kind of take a look at Exhibit 2 and I'll ask you if you've ever seen this report before…and what I'm handing you identified as Exhibit 2 is an OIG Summary of Findings and Conclusions of the investigation into allegations concerning a Green Wall gang at Salinas Valley State Prison. Have you ever seen that document before?" Lanny asked.

Captain Moore stated, "I do not recall seeing this memorandum. Can I keep this?"

"Unfortunately you can't. It's an identified document. Were you ever made aware that a green-handled buck knife had been introduced into the institution?"

"Yes."

"Did you ever see a Salinas Valley State Prison memorandum dated June 5th, 2001 subject- *Introduction of Weapon into Institution*? Did you have any discussions with anyone regarding the introduction of a weapon into the institution?

Moore replied, "Yes, I believe it was with Sergeant Donnahoe."

Lanny asked Moore, "Now, you said you had a meeting with Azell Middlebrooks, Lieutenant Kim, and Sergeant Donnahoe prior to a meeting in which you discipline an employee. This is a meeting with reference to Vodicka, was it discipline as to Vodicka?"

Moore replied, "No."

"How was Vodicka mentioned in this meeting that you had with Middlebrooks, Kim and Donnahoe?"

Moore answered, "He wasn't mentioned specifically. It was the fact that we heard confidential information was being leaked."

Lanny asked, "From whom did you hear that?"

Moore stated, "This is being reported to me…it was the sergeant and lieutenant generally speaking; information was coming back to the supervisors. Confidential information was coming back to them."

Lanny asked in a stern voice, "Did you all consider this to be a problem?"

Moore replied, "Yes."

"And it was this confidential information from ISU… was coming back to you all?" Moore shrugged his head and stated, "Yes."

Lanny began to put the pressure on Moore, "And was there specific confidential

information as it related to Vodicka that was coming back to you, or do you know?"

Moore hesitated for a moment, "Yes."

Lanny asked, "Okay…and what was that?"

Moore replied, "I believe it dealt with a conversation he had with Officer Archibald."

I started to lean forward onto the conference table, this was starting to get very interesting… *was Moore going to tell the truth about the meeting?*

Lanny asked Moore, "Do you recall who it was that told you that Officer Archibald had a conversation with Officer Vodicka and that confidential information had been disclosed by Archibald?"

Moore stared up towards the ceiling, and then his head dropped back down, "Memory serves me right, I believe it was Sergeant Donnahoe who brought to my attention his concerns."

Lanny asked Moore, "How long did this meeting last that you had with Middlebrooks, Kim and Donnahoe?"

"I believe there was one other person there. I just don't know who that fourth person was."

It was Archibald, I thought to myself.

Lanny then asked, "After the meeting you had with that group, did you contact Archibald?"

Moore replied, "Yes."

Lanny reached for the confidential document that I had written to refresh Moore's memory. "Now, at the pre-meeting…I guess…did you have any documents that you were discussing?"

Moore replied, "Yes."

Lanny said, "And do you recall what the document was? I could hand you one."

Moore's face tightened when Lanny placed the stamped *Confidential* document on the table that was prepared by me. Moore replied, "Yes."

Lanny then asked, "What was the document?"

Moore stared right at me and stated, "I believe it was a memorandum authored by Officer Vodicka...and I don't know the gist of it. I wasn't even concerned about what it dealt with. I was only concerned about the area that was highlighted for my attention...and dealt with a comment that Vodicka said that officer Archibald stated to him."

Lanny then replied, "Was there discussion about what you were going to do about the information that had been brought to you from Sergeant Donnahoe?"

Moore replied, "Yes."

Lanny asked, "And what was it that you were going to do?"

Moore started to get very serious, "As to my course of action? My course of action was that—if this is true—that we were going to ask for the resignation of that officer."

"What did you do then? Did the short meeting end and you called Archibald into your office?" Lanny asked.

"Yes, I then stated to Archibald, 'Do you know why you're here?' And I believe he responded, 'No.' I said, 'The reason why you're here is to address some concerns that your supervisor had.' And I went on to inform the officer that our concern, as a unit, is that confidential information was being leaked... and I believe—I'm not sure—but I believe I talked to him about being part of the ISU unit. Every single employee of this unit is considered a confidential employee. So we are privileged to all kinds of confidential information—all of it. It's required that we don't divulge this information outside of that unit. We can talk amongst ourselves because we're held to that level of confidentiality, but you dare not—will not—take this information outside of this unit...and that's clear to everyone that's part of that unit."

Wow, I thought, *this is unbelievable.*

He continued, "I shared that with him to try to get his mind tracking. 'The allegations were that you shared confidential information to an employee outside of this unit.' I believe I made the statement to him that, 'You don't leave me no choice...' and I think that's a direct quote...'You don't leave me no choice but to ask for your resignation."

Lanny had no further questions for Captain Moore.

The deposition of
Sergeant Craig Donnahoe, California Department of Corrections

After Captain Moore's deposition, I stepped outside to take a breath of fresh air. In the parking lot a man stepped out of his truck wearing ragged blue jeans and a long sleeve shirt. His appearance startled me enough to remember I left my gun in the car. As the man slowly approached, I felt foolish: it was my old partner, Craig Donnahoe. Sergeant Craig Donnahoe and I worked together at Pelican Bay State Prison and had transferred at about the same time to Salinas Valley State Prison.

We shook hands; I couldn't believe I didn't recognize him.

"Buddy, I'm not going to lie. I am going to tell the truth about what happened to you."

Lanny began, "Would you characterize Officer Vodicka as being a credible Correctional Officer?"

"Yes, I would."

"Would you consider him to be trustworthy?"

Donnahoe replied, "Yes."

I glanced over at Mary Cain-Simon; she was visibly unnerved by Donnahoe's positive feelings about my character.

"Captain Moore had a report from Vodicka, and Captain Moore was reading from that report. Does that give you a good reference point as to what the meeting was?"

"Yes."

"Where was the meeting?"

"It was in Captain Moore's office."

The Deputy Attorney General interrupted and said sarcastically, "Whew! We've got to go to this meeting."

"I'm trying to help out," Donnahoe said as he shrunk back in his chair.

Lanny came to Donnahoe's defense, "And we appreciate that."

Donnahoe perked back up, "Captain Moore, myself, I believe Robert Kim, he was in, and Steve Archibald,"

Lanny asked, "What did you say?"

Donnahoe stated, "That it was my feelings and my observations that it was time for Steve Archibald to move on—which means, time for him to leave the squad."

Lanny asked, "Why, what did you tell them?"

Cain-Simon interjected, "Okay. If you can get into this without going into any privileged information, please go ahead, or if you can give a general summary."

Donnahoe replied back, "It was due to some of the memos that had come out, I believe. Some remarks that he was making that had come back. My belief that if there was a leak, that it was possibly him."

"Was one of those memos a September 17th memo from D.J. Vodicka— and I'll show it to you refresh your recollection. It's been marked Exhibit 7."

Donnahoe replied back to Lanny, "I believe this is the memo that you are referring to. I know by reading a paragraph what's being spoken to."

Lanny asked, "Which paragraph is that?"

"Second page, third paragraph."

"Why do you recall that paragraph?" Lanny asked.

In a serious tone, Donnahoe replied, "Because it was read to me and others. I believe I told him—Steve Archibald—he had one of two choices: that he could take a weeks vacation until he was reassigned, or he could go ahead and work in the squad for that week until he was reassigned, period. That's it. That was the discussion I had with him."

"So you terminated his assignment from the squad at that point?"

"Yes. If I'm remembering correctly, I left with him—Archibald. I don't want to use the word escort, but I walked with Archibald back to the squad office to have him pack his things."

"Did you have any discussions with him as you walked him out or while he was packing his things?"

Donnahoe looked across the table at me and smiled "Basically he was very, very upset—pissed off, if you will. He was mad as hell at me, at D.J., at Captain Moore, at Lieutenant Kim. The basic feeling that I got, or that was received from him to me was that—you know—it was basically all of our faults that this had happened, that we misinterpreted, misread, misunderstood the facts."

Lanny asked, "Did you say anything in response to his angry statements?"

"Yes. That he needed to shut his mouth and move on and be a man. That's what I told him. Not to upset my staff and my squad any further."

"You said that you subsequently had a meeting with Azell Middlebrooks right after that. What was it about?"

"It was about the information that was divulged by Captain Moore during that meeting with Archibald—that I couldn't believe that Miles Moore did that."

"What was it that you couldn't believe Miles Moore had done?"

"That he had put out there what—the information that he had during the meeting with Archibald that was off of the memo the D.J. Vodicka wrote. And it bothered me that—let's just put it this way—I was in disbelief that the man that was my supervisor of investigations did something like that."

Cain-Simon shifted her weight in her chair. *Ahhh, a little nervous are we now?*

Lanny asked, "Did you consider that to be a breach of some regulation?"

"I consider it to be stupid."

"Would it affect his work environment in some way?"

Donnahoe said, "It could, it could—possibly did. It wasn't necessary. It didn't even need to go there. That's why we had a meeting beforehand. Where we'd already talked about this. I already told him what I wanted to do. He doesn't need to let somebody know the source. Until he started reading from it and my jaw hit the ground and—what the fuck are you doing, was in my mind. It pissed me off that he used that to do what—that didn't need to be done."

Cain-Simon asked Donnahoe, "I think what he wants to know is, did you think that this was going to create trouble for Vodicka besides just being bad for morale, to have employees angry with each other this way?"

What a stupid question. Of course it was going to 'create bad morale,' and that's to say the least.

Angry now, Donnahoe replied, "Yes, I felt that it could be a problem. In many different aspects. We just got done getting rid of a guy for sharing confidential information, and what did we just do to that guy? The same damned thing we've been telling these other people not to do. That's what pissed me off. And it makes me mad right now."

Cain-Simon asked Donnahoe, "Do you want to take another cigarette break?"

"No."

Lanny picked up again, and asked Sergeant Donnahoe, "Did you later have a discussion with Warden Lamarque about what had transpired at this meeting?"

"Yes, sir. Warden Lamarque called me into his office."

"Was there anyone else there besides yourself and Warden Lamarque?"

"I believe Robert Kim may have been there."

"Do you know why he had called you into his office?"

"No. I got called in there all the time for different things—for good things."

"So what happened during that meeting with Warden Lamarque?"

"He asked me if it was true that Miles Moore had read from the memo that D. J. had written—the one that we've been talking about."

"What did you say in response to that?"

"I told him the truth."

"And the truth was, in fact, Miles Moore had read from that memo?"

"Yes, and that he had a look of disbelief on his face. Warden Lamarque, a very professional man, and from what I remember, he didn't show his cards. He didn't say anything."

Lanny asked Donnahoe, "Were you ever made aware that a green-handled buck knife with 723 engraved on the blade was brought into Salinas Valley Prison?"

Donnahoe replied, "Yes."

"Have you ever seen an invoice from an engraving shop in Salinas for the engraving of 723 on the blade?"

Donnahoe replied back, "Yes."

After the deposition, I walked Craig to his car. I knew Mary Cain-Simon didn't like it, but my thoughts on that—*who gives a shit how she feels.*

"Thank you for being honest Craig, you're a true friend. I'm sorry to have put you through all of this."

"I would have done it anyway D. J. You're a great cop, this didn't have to go this way—and they know it."

We shook hands and said good bye.

The deposition of
Correctional Officer Eugene "Gino" Carranza, California Department of
Corrections

Correctional Officer Eugene "Gino" shook my hand the on the day of his deposition. "Great to see you partner. Are you still the number one officer at the prison?" I asked.

Gino replied, "Still number one, but getting ready to retire."

Lanny began by asking Officer Carranza, "What is your understanding the Green Wall?" "My understanding of the Green Wall—I've heard things of situations and incidences that happened on yards."

"Okay—and the things that you heard of, the incidents and things that happened on yard, were those the things that you disclosed in your memo to Greg Lewis?"

Deputy Attorney Mary Cain-Simon immediately interrupted, "Okay. We're talking now, again, about exhibit—do you have a copy of that exhibit here?"

I rolled my eyes; this lady was truly a piece of work.

Gino replied, "No."

Cain-Simon asked Lanny, "Would you hand the witness a copy of Exhibit 4?"

Lanny said, "I want to ask him his memory without looking at Exhibit 4"

Gino said, "Like I said, the incidences that happened on the yard that involved individuals that were partaking in incidences."

Lanny then asked, "When you wrote the memo to Greg Lewis, your line indicates GW. What does that stand for?"

Gino replied, "Green Wall."

"Okay, and then you write that this particular clique is identifiable under the three labels, Green Wall, 7/23 or Code of Silence, what was your understanding of what Green Wall, 7/23 or Code of Silence meant at the time you wrote this memo?"

"Group of individuals who did certain things on different yards."

"What was the 'certain things'"?

"Unlawful."

"Do you recall what yards they were?"

"D and C."

"Taking a look at Exhibit 4, what prompted you to write this memorandum?"

"I was ordered to write this memorandum."

Lanny asked, "By whom?"

Gino replied, "Lewis, Greg Lewis."

I was startled when my phone vibrated inside my jacket. I ignored it.

"Have you ever seen a hand gesture or hand signal associated with the Green Wall?"

"No. But I have been made aware that here is a particular sign that looks like a W."

Lanny indicated the sign across the table to Gino and asked him if he had ever seen the sign.

Gino replied, "Kind of."

"Your memo also sets out that—there is a line here—it says, quote, 'My concern comes only as a direct result from seeing a numerous amount of,'—I think it says—'altercated reports.' What concern did you have there?"

"They were untruthful in their reports."

Lanny said, "And these were individuals associated with the Green Wall?"

Gino responded, "Officers."

Mary Cain-Simon asked for a break. Sure, she wanted this break so she can go outside for some fresh air, before the next questions from Lanny. I hoped Gino would not bite into what she wanted. After the break, Mary Cain-Simon and her client sat back down at the table as Lanny prepared to ask more questions.

Lanny asked Gino, "Do you ever recall a time in which Archibald told Vodicka—and this is in the Sally Port—quote, 'You know that memo you wrote Lieutenant Lewis, that included me in it on the information I gave to you about Lewis taking a state vehicle, etc, and going to see the Regional Administrator?' Do you recall any discussion with D. J. about this?"

"Yes."

"Now, what do you recall of that discussion?"

"D. J. was looking for an answer or looking for something, and he got an answer from Archibald that Lieutenant Lewis left with information to the Regional."

Lanny said, "Now, after that time, was there another encounter between Vodicka and Archibald in the Sally Port, in which Archibald said that he was removed from the squad because of information Vodicka had put in a memo?"

"I remember Archibald being removed from the squad. And I truly don't know or remember the particulars why he was removed, but it was something about a memo."

"Were you ever made aware that Vodicka had been called a snitch by other CDC employees?"

"Yes."

"How were you made aware of this?"

"Well, it's like a grapevine. You hear things."

"This is at the prison, you mean?"

"Yes."

"And when you say it was like a grapevine, did you hear it from a couple of sources?"

Gino replied, "One source."

"From where?"

"The institution that he was working at, someone called him that. It was from the Transportation Office at Pleasant Valley State Prison. I can't remember how the conversation fell into place, but he said, 'Your boy Vodicka, they called him a snitch over there or something at Salinas Valley'. That was the extent of the conversation basically."

My phone began to vibrate again. *Who the hell keeps calling me?*

"Have you ever been called a snitch?"

"Prefer not to answer."

Lanny asked this because when we first opened the prison in 1996, Gino was the chapter president at the prison and he witnessed two supervisors using excessive force on an inmate. Gino reported what he saw and he was labeled a snitch for doing his job.

Lanny asked Gino, "At the time the transportation officer told it to you about what had happened to Mr. Vodicka at Pleasant Valley, was it used in a derogatory way?"

"I believe."

Mary Cain-Simon tried to throw a wrench into the deposition by asking Gino, "When you had that conversation with the transportation officer, had there already been information in the newspapers about Vodicka's lawsuit? Do you recall?"

Gino replied back, "No. He just got there. And D. J. and I worked together and we were friends. And they said, 'Hey, they called your partner, you know, a snitch'. Excuse the language—I said, 'That's fucked up.'"

My phone began to vibrate again, this time I pulled it out to see who was calling me; it was my father. I told Lanny that I had to step outside to take the call. Once outside, my father told me that my mother was not doing well, and suggested I come home as soon as I can.

I went back inside and whispered into Lanny's ear, "I have to leave; my mother is not doing well."

Lanny concluded the deposition with Gino and I immediately got on the road and headed home.

The deposition of
Captain Ryan Williams, California Department of Corrections

A few weeks had past and I received a phone call from Lanny, who told me that the Deputy Attorney General wanted to finish the depositions.

"I am ready to get this done," I told Lanny.

The next day, we are scheduled to hear the testimony from my former boss, Captain Ryan Williams. This was the man that, when I first arrived at Pleasant Valley State Prison after leaving Salinas Valley, made the sarcastic comment toward me saying that I was "the one on the victim witness program they sent here from another prison." He later apologized for his comments and afterward, we actually had a friendly professional relationship.

Lanny and I made it to the conference room. This time, it wasn't Mary Cain-Simon from the Deputy Attorney General's Office, it was a man named Terry Senne. When I first saw Ryan, we both shook each other's hand and politely asked how each other was doing. Ryan was then sworn in by the court reporter and his testimony began.

Lanny asked Captain Williams, "How would you describe your working relationship—in a lot of your testimony—how would you describe your working relationship with D. J. Vodicka?"

Williams replied, "I'd say it was outstanding, because he was a great officer."

Surprisingly, I got choked up after his statement. I took some deep breaths; I wanted to hear what was next.

"What experience did you have with him in order to be able to say that?"

"Because he would take on responsibilities and duties above his own. We had a stabbing in the D facility gymnasium where an inmate was stabbed. I asked D. J. to help me check it out—see what he could come up with. He went to the gymnasium. He interviewed inmates. He looked at all the reports that had already come in. Between the two of us, we reviewed all the reports. We made a determination—we need to talk to the victim, who was in Administration Segregation at that time. D. J. went with me to Administrative Segregation, he got the inmate out of his cell, brought him to the office. Between the two of us interviewing him and pointing out the seriousness of what had happened to him, he identified the assailants. He wrote all the reports on that for me. He didn't—I didn't have to write any reports. He did it all. But it was highly successful. That's just one example."

"So you obviously—did you review—view him as highly credible?"

"D. J.—yes."

"Did you find him trustworthy?"

"I did."

At the conclusion of his deposition, Ryan asked if he could have my cell number to keep in touch. I happily gave it to him.

This would be the last time I would see Ryan. I later found out that Captain Williams had died from a complication during surgery.

The deposition of
Lieutenant Jeffrey Brown, California Department of Corrections

Lieutenant Jeffrey Brown barged into the conference room startling Lanny and me. He seemed rather anxious—hyper and skittish. Lanny told him that he needed to step outside of the room until his counsel arrived; he quickly turned around and just as quickly as he entered, exited the conference room.

"Is that guy on some type of medication?" Lanny asked.

I laughed, "I don't know, he acts like that all of the time—he's just cocky."

A few minutes later, Mary Cain-Simon entered the room, Lieutenant Brown following close behind. *Surely, she coached him on his answers,* I thought.

Lanny asked Lieutenant Brown, "Did you ever have any encounter with officer Vodicka in which it was you, Captain Williams, and Officer Vodicka—the three of you?"

Brown stated, "I used to tour with the facility captain on the facility on a regular basis. Almost daily, and we'd interact, I'm sure many times."

"Did you ever have an interaction with Vodicka in which you made reference to him telling the FBI?"

"Yes. I don't remember the year. It was in the winter—I believe December."

"Do you recall where that was?"

"It was in my office."

"Was anyone else present in the Program Office?"

"I believe it was during shift change. It should have been a lot of second watch and third watch officers, sergeants. A lot of people."

"Were there inmates there?"

"They have inmate clerks that work in the area. They have another office across the hall."

"What did you say to him at that time?"

"I picked—there is a glass between my office and the sergeant's office, and Vodicka was over in the sergeant's office. So I picked up the phone receiver and I tapped on the glass, and I yelled at Vodicka, 'Telephone' and he looked perplexed—wanted to know who it was. And I yelled out it was the FBI. 'They want to know if you want to tell.' I said it quite loudly."

"Did you laugh?"

"Yes."

I was infuriated by his sarcastic, joking tone. *Did he think this was still funny?* I pulled by chair in close to the table, purposely letting it scrape on the ground. According to plan, it got Lieutenant Brown's attention—he turned and looked at me. I stared at him; I wanted him to feel uncomfortable…pressured…I wanted him to see the anger in my eyes.

The deposition of
Warden Anthony Lamarque, California Department of Corrections

"D.J., you ever heard of that saying, 'save the best for last?'"

"Many of times."

"Well, this is going to be an interesting day; Lamarque's testimony is today, under oath."

The deposition took place in a converted hotel room that was made into a conference room. Lanny and I arrived there first, we watched as the videotape technician set up his camera and the court reporter set up her equipment. Mary Cain-Simon entered loudly followed by her client—Warden Anthony Lamarque. Lamarque entered the room wearing a medical belt around his waist and walked slowly, holding a wooden cane. Also following Lamarque into the room was Lieutenant Eloy Medina, from Salinas Valley State Prison. Medina had previously provided statements to the press regarding the Green Wall. Lanny had excused from the deposition because Medina was a witness that Lanny wanted to depose in the future, with regard to his statements about the Green Wall and the changes that Caden and Lamarque had made at the prison.

Lanny asked Lamarque, "Are you on any medication now that will impair your ability to provide your best testimony today?"

Lamarque replied, "I am on medication, but I don't know what the effects are."

"Well, let's go through. What medications are you taking currently?"

"Pain—painkillers, I'm trying to remember the name. I can't remember the name right now."

"Did you take one in the past twelve hours?"

"Yes, numerous."

"And the painkiller is for what condition?"

"For pain, back pain. I had surgery back in late January, I believe."

"Obviously you have the back pain, but does the back pain or any other condition you have impair your ability to provide your best testimony today?"

"No."

"Did you ever discuss the Green Wall with Bill Duncan?"

"Possibility. I'm not really sure. At some—in his capacity as the chief deputy—as the deputy director, but I can't recall."

"What is the Green Wall?" Lanny asked.

"From what I gathered, the Green Wall is like a group of—like a college frat group—I guess, or something like that."

Oh, come on Tony! College frat my ass. Just admit that they work for you and you tell them what to do.

"Are you at all aware that Hickman (Secretary for Corrections) responded, 'I think we have a small minority of people in this agency that have banded together to conceal or attempted to conceal mistakes or acts of misconduct....' And that was Hickman's response to the question 'Is there a Green Wall, Code of Silence in this agency?' Have you ever heard that statement from Hickman?"

Lamarque replied, "No. I don't know if I can answer that question. I can't—I don't—I don't—I don't have an opinion of it. I don't know."

Of course Tony you don't remember something that involves you—you would be incriminating yourself.

"Did you ever have any discussions with Greg Lewis about the Green Wall?"

"Yes."

"How many discussions had you had with Greg Lewis?"

"I can't recall."

"Can you give me an estimate?"

"Four or five—maybe six."

"Now, the one or two phone calls or telephonic discussions that you had with him, what is it you and—I guess it's now Captain Lewis—discussed about the Green Wall? Were there any discussions about staff misconduct?"

"I believe it dealt with some misconduct—I believe."

"In those telephonic discussions that you had with Greg Lewis about the Green Wall, did Greg Lewis express any concern to you that members of the ISU were associated with the Green Wall?"

"Yes."

Lanny asked, "Did you ever discuss the Inspector General's Report about the Green Wall with Ed Alameida?" (Former Director of Corrections)

Lamarque replied, "I can't recall."

"Did you ever see the Inspector General's Report regarding the Green Wall?"

"Yes. Somebody showed it to me—I don't remember."

"Did you have any discussion with that person as to the IG report?"

Lamarque answered, "I don't recall what we talked about, but I'm pretty sure we discussed it."

"Do you agree with the statement that, quote, 'According to Salinas Valley State prison mangers, the warden maintained a relationship with several of the officers assigned to the Investigative Services Unit Security Squad that differed from his relationship with other members of the staff and that may have influenced his actions in relation to those officers,'?"

"I disagree, because I had a good relationship with all my staff."

I shook my head, *bullshit! Then how come the OIG has documented evidence saying otherwise, that you knew of the Green Wall and its members? You sure didn't have a good relationship with me."*

"And the relationship was the same for all staff—is that what you're saying?"

"Yes."

Lanny then asked, "Okay. The next sentence, 'The warden kept the employees relations officer and other managers, out of the loop regarding misconduct investigations and disciplinary issues involving certain members of the Investigative Services Unit Security Squad.' Do you disagree with that?"

"Yes."

"And why is that?"

"Because the people that needed to be involved were involved and were made aware of whatever situation they had to be made aware of."

"So is it your testimony that you kept the ERO (Employee Relations Officer) and other mangers in the loop regarding misconduct investigations and disciplinary issues?"

"Staff that needed to be aware during the time of an investigation is made aware and mangers that were involved were made aware of what was going on," Lamarque responded sharply.

"Did you act on Greg Lewis's report that ISU officers might be involved in the Green Wall?"

"Yes."

"Did Greg Lewis ever report to you or request that you put these officers on temporary reassignment?"

"Greg Lewis did ask me to remove some officers from the unit."

"Did you remove the officers?"

"When he asked me?"

"Yes."

"They were moved at a later time."

"Do you recall there being—or you being made aware of the introduction of a green-handled buck knife with an engraving of 7/23?"

"As of today, yes. I was made aware of a knife being brought in as a gift, yes."

"Other than the discussion you've talked about already—this brief one in your office—did you ever tell Caden that you knew that there were eight boxes of investigative materials at Salinas Valley State prison but you never read them?"

"I told him that I have not read any of the files."

"But you never said, 'I'm sorry. What files are you referring to?'"

Lamarque stated, "The files in question that we're talking about, when you said 'Have you ever read the investigative files' I said no."

"And these were the Investigative files regarding the Green Wall?"

"Correct."

"Was there a reason you never read them?" Lanny asked.

"Yes. The department was doing it and they told me—you know—stay out of it, they will handle it, so I just let them do it."

You're the friggin' warden of the prison; you're supposed to know everything going on at the prison.

"Who at the department told you to stay out of it?"

Lamarque said, "I can't recall who was in charge at the time, but I was told by—to stay out of it and just let the department handle all the aspects of that."

"Now, as the warden, do you have responsibility for the Security Squad?"

"Yes. The whole prison. But the squad—Investigative Unit—falls under me, yes."

"So are you responsible for the assignment of officers to the unit and then the removal of officers from the unit?

"Yes, in a way."

"Do you recall asking Donnahoe what happened at the meeting between Miles Moore and Steve Archibald?"

"Good possibility."

"Do you recall asking Craig Donnahoe whether Miles Moore had shown Vodicka's September 17th memo to Archibald?"

"I believe so."

Suddenly, the Deputy Attorney General asked if she could take a brief break to have a quick talk with the next witness.

O, of course you do. Here we go again.

When she returned back into the room she stated, "It has been brought to my attention—during the break I should say—that there is a reporter waiting outside to take Mr. Lamrque's picture. I'd like to take a break in the deposition to ask the hotel staff to escort the gentleman off the premises. But, Mr. Tron, I just want to say this is the most discourteous and unprofessional act by an attorney I have ever encountered, that you would summon a photographer to harass—to harass the witness who has appeared for a deposition in a litigated case."

Lanny and I had nothing to do with the reporter being there.

Lanny fired back, "Let me just advise counsel that there is no need for a subpoena. He is an employee. You agreed to produce him. I appreciate that we have taken the deposition. The reporters can do what the reporters want to do. I can't control a reporter Ms. Simon, and you're quite aware of that. They are people who have the right to do whatever they want to do. And if they choose to take a picture of Mr. Lamarque in a public place, I can't prevent them from doing that."

Deputy Attorney General Cain-Simon stated, "The deposition is terminated."

Lanny shouted back, "No, it's not done—and we are not off the record!"

Ms. Cain-Simon stormed out of the room leaving Mr. Lamarque sitting in his chair all alone. The door was wide open; a reporter entered and asked Mr. Lamarque if he could take a picture of him. Mr. Lamarque jumped out of his chair and began to swing his cane towards the reporter's camera, coming close to striking him in the face. The reporter took several pictures of him, while Mr. Lamarque made his way to the door.

When Deputy Attorney General Cain-Simon entered the room, she was extremely agitated. She told us that the deposition with Lamarque was terminated and that she would not produce him again.

Lanny said, "I am not finish with Mr. Lamarque and we are not done with this deposition."

Mr. Lamarque stormed out of the room trying to balance on the cane.

Lanny went to Judge Fields to inform him that the Deputy Attorney General stopped our scheduled deposition with Lamarque. Judge Fields ordered Deputy Attorney General Cain-Simon to produce Mr. Lamarque for more deposition testimony. Mary Cain-Simon advised Judge Fields that she could not produce Mr. Lamarque for next week's deposition because she stated, "Mr. Lamarque left the country to France and did not know how to contact him."

Subsequently, Mr. Lamarque never showed for the continuance of his testimony in our scheduled deposition. Lanny and I later found out that Mr. Lamarque returned back to the United States *after* the Department of Corrections settled my case.

The next day the photograph of Lamarque was in the newspaper,—the article titled, *Raising cane- Former prison warden tries to smite pesky reporter.* According to Terry Francke, an attorney with Californians Aware—a nonprofit organization that works to strengthen open-government laws—said that the reporter was completely within his rights to go to the hotel and attempt to interview subjects and take pictures. Francke explained that a hotel was a public place. Although a reporter may have no right to barge into a deposition while it is in session, the hallway outside the conference room was not much different from a public sidewalk.

Francke finished with, "The problem is; when a Deputy Attorney General takes it upon herself to declare a reporter nuisance, what she really means is that she doesn't want him to cover the story."

Chapter Eighteen

Closure

I drove down to Redding, California to find a realtor to look at some property in the Shasta Mountain area. After a few days of house-hunting, I returned back to the realtor's office for another search. I was taken aback when she asked me if I knew of a lady named Mary Cain-Simon from the Attorney General's Office. Apparently Cain-Simon called the realtor asking questions about me— if I was a threat to her—the realtor—if I showed my badge and questioned what I was going in the area.

I immediately called Lanny to let him know I was being followed—how else would she know where I was?

"Stay in your hide-out until I get this resolved."

I headed back to the cabins in the mountains, where I informed Mary Ann what had taken place.

I received a call from Marian—my girlfriend who I had met while visiting my parents in Arizona—telling me that my father was in the hospital. My mother was battling cancer and was told she had a year to live; I was shocked to hear my father had fallen ill too.

It was late July, 2005; the weather was scorching hot when I arrived in Arizona a day later. After several tests, my father was diagnosed with stomach cancer—peritoneal adeno csrcinomztosis. The doctor said he had less that month to live.

A week later, On August 2, 2005, I learned Sergeant James George's charges where sustained. My case number was *04-0624E of Donald J. Vodicka*, *"Of whistleblower retaliation in the position of Correctional Officer with Salinas Valley State Prison, Department of Corrections and Rehabilitation at Salinas.* Judge Horst made the following order to the pursuant to the foregoing findings of fact and issues:

In order to establish a claim for whistleblower retaliation, a complaint must demonstrate, by a preponderance of evidence, that having made a protected disclosure was a contributing factor in retaliatory action taken against him or her. If a complainant meets this burden, the burden then shifts to the respondent to demonstrate by clear and convincing evidence that the action would have occurred for legitimate, independent reasons even if the complainant had not made a protected disclosure. Government Code 8547.3 defines unlawful retaliation as follows: An employee may not directly or indirectly use or attempt to use the official authority or influence of the employee for the purpose of intimidating, threatening, coercing, commanding or attempting to intimidate, threaten, coerce or command any person for the purpose of interfering with the rights conferred pursuant to this article. In addition to an outright threat, intimidation, or coercion, the courts have found retaliation where the employee can show, by a preponderance of the evidence, that he suffered an adverse employment action due to his protected activity. George was aware that complainant had filed a lawsuit against Archibald. The lawsuit related to complainant's protected disclosures about a "green wall." George specifically referenced the lawsuit and then told complainant to "back off." George, however, is a supervisor and his conduct was inappropriate. It is concluded that, based on the totality of the circumstances, a Letter of Instruction advising George against such action is an appropriate corrective measure.

I was furious. According to the new matrix that was set in place for discipline measures by the Federal Courts for the Department of Corrections, a harsher penalty should have been given to Sergeant George. A Letter of Instruction is like a "slap on the hand." The letter is removed from his personal file after one year.

Twelve days later, my father passed away on August 14, 2005.

I stayed home that summer to take care of my ailing mother. I knew she was lonely without my dad. She passed away on Valentines Day, February 14, 2006. I never got to say goodbye to her, but I knew that was ok. She would have responded with, "We never say goodbye. We say until we meet again."

❦　　❦　　❦

My case never went to trial. It was settled out of court by the California Department of Corrections. In the settlement, the California Department of Corrections wanted me to voluntary resign from the department and after, they would not contest my disability retirement and Workers Compensation case. They also did not want me to return to any state service employment—basically, they just wanted to pay me off and disappear.

On April 13, 2006, I received a letter from Thelton E. Henderson, Senior United States District Judge from the United States District Court in San Francisco, California. Judge Henderson was overseeing the California Department of Corrections and Rehabilitation from a federal standpoint along with Special Master John Hagar. Both men oversaw one of the most important cases against the California Department of Corrections—Madrid vs. California Department of Corrections. The Madrid case was brought on by Pelican Bay State Prison. The letter contained the following:

> *Thank you for your recent letter of support. The Special Master appointed for the Madrid litigation, John Hagar, has been keeping me informed about your personal situation, including the retaliation you suffered after submitting reports concerning the Green Wall at Salinas Valley State Prison. At Mr. Hagar's advice, I decided to wait to respond to your previous letter until your state court litigation had concluded. I understand that your case has now been resolved through a settlement agreement.*
>
> *I want to assure you, I intend to continue vigorously monitoring the California Department of Corrections and Rehabilitation's handling of Code of Silence and investigative/ discipline issues.*
>
> *The Court's remedial plans would not have been possible if it were not for correctional employees, like yourself, who have the courage to stand up against the Code of Silence. I want to emphasize to you personally that I have the upmost respect for the position that you took, and sympathy concerning the many adverse consequences that resulted. Mr. Hagar and I wish you the very best for the future.*
>
> *Signed by Judge Thelton E. Henderson*

❦　　❦　　❦

I believe the California Department of Corrections has lost its integrity and ability to police itself. Complete structural reform from top to bottom is needed. The people and their elected or appointed leaders are who give meaning to the value of the piece of paper on which any policy is written. If top officials neither understand nor care about the need for fair investigations, they are unlikely to investigate thoroughly or will investigate with prejudice.

A Code of Silence is no stranger to the prison system, but there is a fine line between influence and intimidation. When the oath we took before starting our career in law enforcement is compromised, we are tested—do we stand up in the pursuit of justice or do we cower and fall under intimidation?

I am proud to know my feet never left the ground.